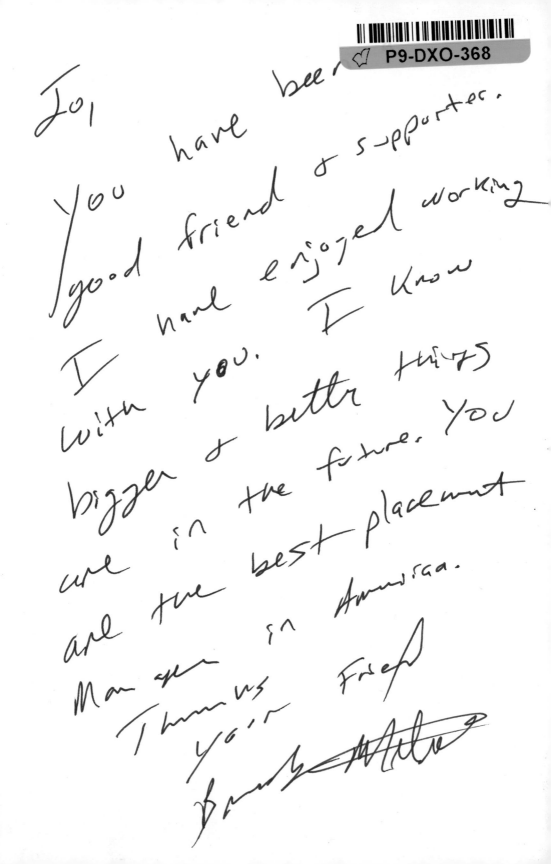

Jo,

You have been a good friend & supporter. I have enjoyed working with you. I know bigger & better things are in the future. You are the best placement Manager in America. Thanks your Friend

BET ON COWBOYS, NOT HORSES

BROOKS MITCHELL, Ph.D.

York Publishing Co.
Shaker Heights, Ohio 44120

Library of Congress Cataloging-in-Publication Data 93-060890
Mitchell, James Brooks, Ph.D.

Bet On Cowboys, Not Horses.
A Technological Breakthrough for Employee Selection

Includes bibliographical references.
ISBN 0-9634940-2-3
1. Employee selection   2. Front-line hiring
I. Title

Cover design: Roberta Dickinson
Interior design: Pioneer Printing

Printed in the United States of America.

10 9 8 7 6 5 4 3 2 1   93-06089C
                                                              CIP

You can't bring the cows in without a couple of good hands. I'm fortunate to have two of the best: Danny Rue Thomas, a cowgirl and no relation to The Danny Thomas, and Even Brande, a cowpoke. They spent countless hours organizing and attending to all the details. I'm a very lucky rancher to have them on the ranch.

DEDICATION

To the memory of Mable Grace Apple

CONTENTS

INTRODUCTION

"I have nothing to lose, so I'll speak my mind."

Billy Joe Minyard

Let me begin with a simple statement. In order for today's corporations to win the intense battle of competition, they must efficiently choose and effectively use the right people at the front line of their organizations.

Companies spend millions of dollars finding the "right" employees to fill top management positions but often give short shrift to the task of hiring the right people the first time for lower-level job openings.

Hiring and keeping the right people can make a huge difference in your firm's competitiveness and ultimate level of success. The trend toward industry consolidation and intensifying global competition make it harder than ever to sell your goods and services in both domestic and international markets. They also heat up the competition for qualified employees who actually give a damn about their jobs and your firm's productivity.

Work Place 2000, a government-sponsored study, listed finding qualified employees as a major challenge facing American companies as we move toward the twenty-first century.

You can no longer afford to conduct your hiring operations "as usual." It's time to enter the twenty-first century by using technology and employee selection techniques that are guaranteed to improve your firm's hiring success, cut human resource costs, and improve your bottom line through improved productivity and reduced employee turnover.

That's what you can accomplish by sitting back, listening to my advice, and putting my proven, employee selection tools into practice. It's a tall order, but with more than twenty years of employee selection research and, more importantly, practical experience in helping top North American companies streamline their hiring processes, I can improve the efficiency and effectiveness of your firm's hiring operation. I stake my reputation on it.

My firm, Aspen Tree Software, Inc., specializes in making the best better. From our offices in Laramie, Wyoming, we use state-of-the-art technology that is the envy of much larger companies. We will show you how to use this technology in tandem with proven employee selection techniques to significantly enhance your firm's hiring of front-line employees.

I have written this book so that it would be both informative and fun to read. It is intended to be based equally upon solid employment research, the practical implications and applications of the research, and good common sense. And, of course, the book is liberally sprinkled with the unparalleled sagacity of the American Cowboy. I have learned to have a deep respect for the wisdom and unvarnished insight of a cowboy. A real cowboy knows a bunch about hiring and keeping good people on the payroll.

Picking up a copy of **Bet on Cowboys, Not Horses** and investing a little time in reading it and applying its message could be the best business decision you make this year.

Good reading, trail bosses.

Bubba & B.J.
Cowboy tips on employee selection

The bigger the hat, the smaller the ranch.

CHAPTER ONE

BET ON COWBOYS, NOT HORSES

*"When the dust clears, a good cowboy will always
ride a good horse."*
Bubba Joe

Why the title, **Bet On Cowboys, Not Horses**? The philosophy originates from a legend etched into the heart and soul of Wyoming. It is exemplified by the greatest bronco ride that ever was. The day in 1909 when a cowboy named Clayton Danks climbed on a wild bronco named Steamboat . . . what an afternoon it must have been. It featured nothing less than the best cowboy trying to ride the baddest dang mustang in all of Wyoming. Days before the famous ride took place, the word spread like wildfire on the telegraph wires across ranches from Montana to Colorado. Cowboys from all over the West rode miles of dusty trails to witness the ride.

It represented the classic match, the best agin' the best: Frazier against Ali, the Dodgers against the Yankees, and Laver against Rosewall. Nothing less than the designation of world champion bronco rider was at stake. It matched the cowboy that had never been throwed with the hoss that had never been rode.

When Danks finally climbed on Steamboat and dug his spurs in, an eruption that would embarrass Vesuvius occurred. Steamboat took Danks on the wildest ride that any cowboy ever experienced before or since. Nearly ninety years later people still talk about that historic day and people like me can't quit writing about it. All Wyoming school kids learn about the ride before they learn about George Washington and the cherry tree and Honest Abe's log cabin. Steamboat and Danks are embossed on every license plate and official state document, even marriage licenses. Clayton Danks on Steamboat symbolizes the determination, independence, and soul of Wyoming. They represent the best against the best: the cowboy who couldn't be thrown on the horse that couldn't be rode.

It all took place in 1909 at Cheyenne Frontier Days, the Granddaddy of all rodeos. Even today, the nation's top cowpunchers consider the Cheyenne Rodeo as the World Series of rodeos. If you can ride in Cheyenne, you can ride anywhere.

As reported in the journals of the day, "Danks sat firmly in his saddle before the chute handlers released Steamboat from his blindfold. As usual, the outlaw took a good look around before commencing proceedings, then up went his back into an arch like an angry cat, his tail went behind his hind legs and he began giving Danks the ride of the century. Steamboat hurtled from the chute with a wicked twist characteristic of the worst horses."

Clayton Danks on Steamboat, Cheyenne Frontier Days, 1909. *(Photograph: Courtesy of the American Heritage Center, Univ. of Wyoming)*

Danks knew he had mounted a runaway locomotive. There was nothing to do but hang on. Later, he told the Cheyenne Frontier Times, "I had my head snapped back until I thought it was going to come off, and I felt as if my lungs were going to burst when I had ridden that horse for a few jumps. He was bucking pretty hard, too hard to grab the horn; he tore me loose from there ... he went around and around. He threwed me over here and over there and this way and that and a many a time I thought, 'Well, here I go'."

Danks must have sensed the significance of the ride. To the awe of all in attendance, he took off his hat and fanned Steamboat. It was the touch that sealed the legend forever. When it was over and the dust cleared, Steamboat wasn't movin' ... and Danks still sat firmly in the saddle. In the air and falling dust, old Steamboat was "a heavin'." Then the cowboys started to cheer and offer the ultimate tribute of tossin' their hats into the dirt at the hoofs of Steamboat. They all knew they had witnessed something they would never see again: a clash of the Titans, two Greek heroes in a fight to the death.

That's how it is in business. A good salesperson can sell an average product. A poor salesperson cannot sell a good product. Remember, nothing sells itself. Bet on salespeople, not products!

A good engineer makes a project work. A poor engineer dooms a great project to delays, malfunctions, and ultimate failure. Bet on engineers, not projects!

A positive store salesclerk sells to a marginally-interested customer while a negative clerk seldom sells to a positive shopper. Bet on the clerks, not the customers!

Venture capitalists have known this lesson for years. Sure, they would rather have an A product with an A management team. But, if they have to choose between an A product with a B management team or a B product with an A management team, they will choose the latter every time. People make the difference, not products and designs.

Clayton Danks and Steamboat represent Wyoming. They represent what we believe at Aspen Tree Software, Inc. People make the difference. No matter how good our software is or how much it saves our many users, if we can't add the critical human element, it won't work. Any savvy programmer can duplicate what we do once they understand our methodology and techniques.

Yet if we've got the right people with the right attitude, that can never be duplicated. With the right people, we meet challenges and overcome obstacles that intimidate and eliminate our imitators. Our people make the difference. We can ride the wildest horses.

Therein lies the challenge to America's businesses: Ride the horses that others won't mount. We must not be afraid of our competitors. Rather, we must understand that we ultimately win our battles with our people, not our technology. In the end, good cowboys always ride a good horse. Clayton Danks did.

This book is not about hiring managers; it deals with hiring people at the front line, people who do the work. It will help you to hire the best front-line employees. It is dedicated to the single principle that in today's global economy, more than ever, front-line employees make the difference.

This book focuses on identifying and hiring those folks who keep your business running like a well-oiled machine on a day-to-day basis. In other words, it targets those troops in the trenches who meet and deal every day with your customers and suppliers.

This book is about those back office or plant personnel who work behind the scenes to make sure orders get filled, products get made and shipped, and customer service gets provided right, the first time. It's about people who actually like their work and care about doing a good job.

The days of easy productivity gains due to technology breakthroughs are over. Those companies that know how to identify, find, and hire the best employees will be the ones who prosper and grow, and will be able to maintain a significant competitive edge bolstered by higher productivity, reduced employee turnover, and a committed team of dedicated employees.

By reading **Bet on Cowboys, Not Horses**, you will understand how to locate and hire the best front-line employees for your business. To be sure, there are plenty of pitfalls in the front-line employment process. For example, a recent study found that one-third of all job applicants lied about job experience. And there are thousands of 'snake oil' remedies along the employee selection path. They don't work! Like the cowboys in Wyoming say, "If it don't make sense, don't believe it." However, the good news is that there are two (only two) proven solutions that work in the area of front-line selection: the structured job interview and the company- and job-specific criterion validity study. In the chapters that follow, I will discuss these successful hiring techniques and associated topics in detail.

Don't expect a quick fix or magic solution to the employee selection dilemma. There isn't one. If you are expecting to discover an easy solution, you will be disappointed. There is no pill you can take which will lift the scales from your eyes and reveal the perfect job applicant.

Good employee selection involves hard work and persistence, but the payoff is worth it. If you want a pill, go to the medicine cabinet and get one and return this book for a full refund. Then call Madame Swami the Seer and ask her to consult her Tarot cards; or you might try a spin of the roulette wheel. Either of these solutions will yield similar results. However, if you seek to improve your company's employee selection program with solid, proven techniques, read on. I promise, you'll get your money's worth.

You may ask, "Why do I need to read about employee selection? My firm already staffs a human resource department whose duty is to interview and hire people." That's a legitimate question. Let me explain it this way. First of all, most human resource managers spend the majority of their selection time and effort on recruiting and hiring key managers and executives. That's more exciting and thus gets more attention. This book is not about filling top or middle management positions. It's about the unique problems and solutions of front-line hiring of the other key people, those employees who make it all come together.

Second, most human resource people dedicated to front-line hiring almost always fall into the junior manager ranks and frequently lack the skill and knowledge required to hire optimally at the front line. Even if they did possess the necessary skills and tools, their junior status frequently precludes them from gaining the ear and confidence of upper managers. Furthermore, my years of experience and observation point out that most organizations reward front-line interviewers for quantity hiring, not quality hiring. This is reflected in reports that emphasize such measurements as the number of days a job was open before it was filled or the number of interviews per hire. Under these circumstances, junior interviewers quickly get the message and understand the source of their organizational rewards: "Fill jobs!"

Making the situation even worse, junior interviewers are frequently unproved in the organization and many of them may not be up to the top standards; thus, you may be in a situation where sub-performing people are making critical hiring and screening decisions. There's truth in the saying, "First-rate people hire first-rate people, and second-rate people hire third-rate people."

Third, hiring at any level of the organization cannot be optimal if it is perceived as an exclusive human resource function. Line managers must be involved every step of the way. They must bear the ultimate accountability for the hiring decision, not the human resource interviewer.

Finally, many managers perceive front-line interviewing as dull and monotonous work and, therefore, few like to do it. Consequently, this vital task usually gets relegated to new human resource managers. That's how it operated at Texas Instruments when I worked there in the mid-sixties. In those days we were literally hiring hundreds of people a day. We would tell new and eager personnel employees, "First you start off in the non-exempt employment area. If you survive and don't quit, we'll promote you to the exciting and enriching job of employee records manager." And upper management wonders why turnover continues.

Bet On Cowboys, Not Horses is built on a foundation of solid academic research. It reflects years of personal and professional training, education, and experience. As an educator, I always remain the skeptic. I demand to see the proof of studies published in the most rigorous independent journals. Yet, academic research in the area of employee selection must ultimately deliver practical application to organizations to be meaningful.

How can we implement or benefit from the conclusions reached by the studies? That's how I attacked this crucial area of employee selection.

Pre-employment screening has never been and never will be a precise science; but this book documents two proven concepts which can significantly improve your percentage of successful front-line hires. They are the structured job interview and the company- and job-specific criterion validity study. Furthermore, it shows how to effectively use a computer to synergistically combine the structured job interview with the criterion validity study.

My goal is to blend the implications of decades of employee selection research with the real world, the arena in which your firm competes each and every day. I'll interpret and explain what it all means and how to apply it to your organization. I'll point out problem areas and pitfalls encountered by firms who do not take a proven approach to their front-line employee selection techniques.

I am uniquely qualified in the field of employee selection for four reasons. First, I have a strong academic background in the area of front-line employee selection. This interest was kindled during my early days as a practicing human resource manager for Texas Instruments and PepsiCo. I witnessed firsthand and dealt with the massive problems inherent in hiring volumes of assembly operators and truck drivers.

At Texas Instruments we hired hundreds of people a day. Mass confusion reigned and the results were inevitable. We would hire someone, and he or she would be gone two weeks later. I ran into similar situations at PepsiCo while hiring truck drivers for North American Van Lines and National Trailer Convoy. We conducted an annual giant hiring venture and it proved less than optimum. I remember having to explain to a Marine General how we had lost his entire truck of personal possessions and furniture and his question, "How do you lose a truck? I understand how you might lose a car. I don't understand how you lose an entire truck!" The answer was simple. The driver had left the truck someplace and walked off. We had hired the wrong person.

I knew there must be a better way to hire the best qualified employees. Eventually, this evolved into my doctoral dissertation at The University of North Texas. Most doctoral dissertations begin with a hypothesis that may or may not solve a problem. In my case, the reverse proved to be true. I knew what the problem was and I began searching for a solution. For me, it was a quest for the Holy Grail: to discover what really worked in the important area of front-line hiring. My discoveries and conclusions, derived from years of research, form an important part of this book.

Second, my real-world work experience at Texas Instruments and PepsiCo is invaluable. It provides a reality check I constantly rely on. There is no substitute for battle experience: learning what works and what doesn't work, first hand. My work experience allows me to decipher and mitigate much of the academic fog that exists in the field of front-line employee selection.

There are reams and volumes of research conclusions. I know which conclusions have practical application and which do not. We will discuss those studies which pass the acid test of transition from the ivory tower to the trenches, providing practical meaning and application in the quest for optimized front-line hiring.

Third, I have spent twenty years in independent work helping with many of America's largest corporations with the implementation of front-line employee selection systems. My client list includes such firms as American General Corporation, Exxon, General Tire, Kaiser Permanente, Marriott, American Express, Neiman Marcus, Foley's, Mrs. Field's Cookies, and many others. My employee selection techniques have been documented by these companies to improve hiring efficiency, enhance front-line employee performance, reduce employee turnover, improve customer service, and in some cases, decrease employee theft.

The 1991 annual report for the American General Corporation states: "Since the implementation of a computer-assisted employment interview, our agent turnover decreased by eight percent." Most companies also report that they have been able to streamline and make their hiring procedures more consistent while improving their applicant-to-hire ratios. **Bet On Cowboys, Not Horses** will teach you how to benefit from the experience and success of these companies, and, more importantly, how to duplicate the impressive results in your own company.

Fourth, I practice what I preach. I have used my hiring knowledge and experience to build Aspen Tree Software, Inc., into a team of fiercely dedicated, knowledgeable, and productive employees. Just as the concepts in this book promote the full use of available technology in the hiring process, I take advantage of technology at Aspen Tree.

Technological changes create even larger social changes. That has clearly been the case at Aspen Tree Software, Inc. Currently, there are fourteen employees, all of whom work full-time, earning good livings while pursuing their careers from the comfort of their own homes. We're all connected by computers, file servers, networks, and faxes. Many of our associates are mothers with pre-school children who are able to work while being instantly available to their children.

It's not that I am such a nice guy, a man of the nineties, that I let Aspen Tree Software associates work from home. No, it is much more basic than that. I am thoroughly convinced that where it is possible, these employees are far more productive at home than if I required them to come to the corporate office (which, incidentally, is my home).

Occasionally, someone will ask me, "How do you know these people are working?" My response never varies, "I don't, but if I've got the right cowgirls and cowboys, the job will get done." The secret to letting people work at home lies in hiring the right person and then managing the job, not the person.

A vital premise of this book is that every company possesses its own unique work environment and set of success factors, and that a successful front-line employment process must reflect those differences. In fact, different divisions, departments, and facilities within the very same company often exhibit a wide variety of work environments and success factors. A selection criteria that works for one company will not work for another. In other words, there are no magic questions that can be asked of all applicants for all jobs. It's not that simple. A good interview question for your company may be a poor one for another company, or even for a different division within your organization.

The real trick lies in learning to identify good questions and criteria specific to your company: criteria which select employees who will stay with you as productive members of the organization. It does your firm no good to hire good people this year, only to see them leave your employ six months to a year down the road. Likewise, it's foolish to hire 'bodies' that won't grow in experience and productivity. Remember, the same experience for twenty years does not constitute twenty years of experience.

As an analogy, **Bet On Cowboys, Not Horses** demonstrates how a Hershey's™ Chocolate Bar (structured job interview) can be combined synergistically through a computer with Skippy's™ Peanut Butter (criterion validity study) to create a Reese's™ Peanut Butter Cup, the best thing you can ever lock a lip on. (See Chapter Nine.)

While all of this may sound complicated, it really isn't difficult. There are two concepts that work:

1) The structured job interview and 2) The criterion validity study. They affect three critical stages in improving your selection process: finding, selecting and keeping employees.

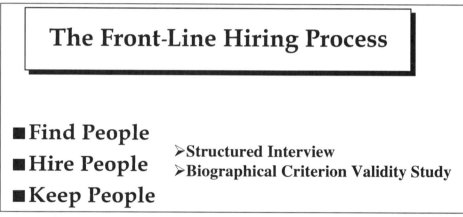

The Front-Line Hiring Process

■ **Find People**

■ **Hire People** ➢**Structured Interview**
➢**Biographical Criterion Validity Study**

■ **Keep People**

Figure 1-1

That doesn't seem too difficult, does it?

Within these pages you will find real world examples, employee selection research, practical case studies, and down-to-earth advice on how to put it all together: how to make the process in Figure 1-1 work for you — how to bet on cowboys, not horses.

Our procedures and ideas have stood the test of time. It has been over fifteen years since I first tried the process of using a computer to conduct a pre-employment interview. It has been a long but rewarding journey from the use of a simple Apple II computer hooked to a Radio Shack cassette recorder to the marvelous computers that we use today.

It has not always been easy and I have suffered my share of slings and arrows. I have found that as you plow new ground and break from tradition and conventional wisdom, you travel through three very distinct phases in the eyes of your peers.

Phase I: You are ridiculed and humored for your off-the-wall ideas.

Phase II: You are violently opposed as you persist, and your ideas take root.

Phase III: At last, you are widely accepted as being self-evident.

I have to be honest; I like phase III the best. The computer-aided employee selection techniques I developed are now soundly in the widely-accepted phase. Aspen Tree Software has helped many of America's top companies improve their employee selection techniques with an accompanying rise in employee productivity and a decrease in employee turnover. It is this demand for better employee selection information that led to the writing of this book and testifies to the fact that we are on the right trail.

Why the title, Bet On Cowboys, Not Horses?–because too many companies hire employees with the mistaken belief that they will change once they are on the payroll, that the organization or the job somehow will exude a force that will compensate for any shortcomings the new employee possesses. Wrong! It works exactly the other way. A marginal employee will contaminate a good job or organization. Remember, a rotten apple spoils the barrel. A thousand good apples cannot firm up the rotten one. To increase the frequency of winning, bet on the cowboy, not the horse.

Clayton Danks on Steamboat
The Symbol of the Great State of Wyoming

CHAPTER TWO

THE HUMAN NATURE FACTOR

THE WILD SIDE OF LIFE

I'd write you a letter but you wouldn' read it.
You asked me not to call you on the phone.
But there's somethin' I've got to tell you,
So I wrote it in the words of this song.

The glamour of the gay night life has lured you
To the places where the wine and liquor flow
Where you wait to be anybody's darlin'.
You gave up the truest love you'll ever know.

I didn't know God made Honky Tonk Angels.
I might of knowed you'd never make a wife.
You gave up the only one that ever loved you
And went back to the wild side of life.

By Hank Thompson, a love sick cowboy

"The Wild Side Of Life," one of the greatest and most poignant honky tonk songs ever written, says it all: Once a honky tonk angel, always a honky tonk angel. All the love that Hank gave that woman didn't change her. He met her in a bar and she is still there today. People don't change!

Or, if they do change, it takes intervention at a higher level than most managers work. The only significant character change I am aware of is recorded in the Bible, in the 26th chapter of Acts.

"On one such occasion I was traveling toward Damascus armed with the authority and commission of the chief priests. On this journey . . . I saw a light more brilliant than the sun shining in the sky at midday. It surrounded me . . . all of us fell to the ground and I heard a voice saying to me in Hebrew, 'Saul, Saul, why do you persecute me?' . . . I could not disobey that heavenly vision . . . I preached a message of reform."

Saul showed good judgment and cleaned his act up on the spot. He permanently changed his character and went forth doing good. Unfortunately, I have never heard of a similar conversion in business. Human character doesn't change and anybody who believes it does should be working for a social agency, not a profit-oriented business.

Consider the following story of an employer attempting to change character traits and the situation that ensued. A few years back when the federal government ran its CETA (Civilian Employment Training Administration) program, a buddy of mine decided to avail himself of the benefits offered. He went to the CETA office and filled out the required reams of paperwork (the federal bureaucracy in action) in order to hire a CETA applicant for his muffler replacement and automotive repair business. On the surface, the deal looked like one that any prudent businessperson and conscientious citizen could ill afford to resist.

Under the CETA program, the government picked up the tab for the training wage and one-half of the employee's wages for up to six months after the training period ended. With labor costs accounting for over fifty percent of a standard muffler replacement job, the wage reimbursement proved to be a major incentive to enter into a contract with the local CETA office. In addition, good ol' Uncle Sam would supply the CETA employee with a full set of the mechanic's tools required to perform the automotive repair work, another substantial cost savings.

The only concern stemmed from the fact that the proposed CETA employee was a young teenager fresh from the state reform school. The CETA administration would check weekly on the employee's attendance, progress, etc., to ensure that no problems were arising. The young man also had a strong incentive to perform. Unless he abided by his parole restrictions (such as no drinking) and

13

performed a satisfactory job at work, he would be returned to reform school.

It looked like a win/win/win situation. The kid would get a second chance to become a productive member of society. The government and taxpayers would reap a benefit in lower costs to house and feed a law breaker plus derive additional taxes from the CETA employee's wages. Finally, my automotive shop owner buddy would gain a productive employee, trained at government expense and subsidized for half a year. Really, how can you beat a deal like that?

It looked perfect on paper, and at first it worked just like it was originally laid out. The kid possessed a knack for working on cars and quickly picked up the necessary skills to perform good repair work. The government wage reimbursement checks arrived right on schedule, helping to cut costs and improve cash flow. The CETA administrator showed up regularly to check on the employee's progress and to inquire about any problems or concerns of either the employee or my friend. But you have heard the saying, "The best laid plans of mice and men often go astray."

This situation began to unravel one evening when the CETA employee decided to take a customer's car, which had been left overnight for repair the next day, for a joy ride. The joy ride included a stop at the local liquor store. Fortunately, the owner of the car saw his vehicle at the liquor store and called the police. After a brief pursuit, the police apprehended the employee and put him in jail. While the car owner was justifiably miffed, the overall damage was limited to embarrassment. However, think of the legal and business consequences if the employee had gotten drunk and smashed up the customer's vehicle, or worse, killed somebody in a traffic accident. To make a long story short, the kid went back to prison, this time to the big house, and my friend paid more attention to character in the future. You can't make chicken salad out of chicken kaw kaw, and people don't change.

In *The Motivation To Work* (John Wiley & Sons, 1959), Fredrick Herzberg, Bernard Mausner from Beaver College in Pennsylvania, and Barbara B. Snyderman of the University of Pittsburgh School of Medicine brought new insight into the research of job attitudes, motivation, and productivity. One of the key conclusions to come from this research work is that companies must not only look to restructuring the job in order to motivate employees with meaningful goals, they must also restructure the employee selection process. Included in that employee selection process is the requirement to attempt to analyze the potential abilities of the applicant for work. This goes beyond an analysis of the ability to perform work tasks (which can be taught) to the realization that there are combinations of abilities and temperaments that will lead to success in the same job for different reasons.

Based on extensive research and years of practical industry experience, I remain firmly convinced that you can't train character. A person's character traits are set early in life. If you concentrate too much on specific work experience, you can fall into the trap of hiring the wrong person for your job position. Again, thirty years performing the same job does not equate to thirty years of experience. In other words, you can train employees to run a cash register, but you can't train them to care about customers. They either care or they don't. You can educate salespeople about a product, but you can't teach them how to sell if they don't have the basic sales characteristics. This raises the obvious question, "Then why do we train people how to sell, or why do we train for customer service?" Good question! I think this falls into the analogy of coaching. For example, a person with musical aptitude can be coached to play a piano. A person with no musical aptitude can never be trained to play a piano. In business, a salesperson who likes people can be coached to be better at customer service, but you can't train a person to love selling or to love helping customers. It either is there or it isn't.

With this in mind, we at Aspen Tree Software develop our employee selection software programs to weed out, through the biographical criterion validity study, those job applicants likely to possess character traits that have proven detrimental to employee success within a particular company environment. Key success factors in one company's scenario may prove to contribute to employee failure at another company with a different corporate culture. For example, numerous retailing studies have shown that college education in some retail organizations can be related to success while in others it cannot. I suspect the difference depends on the company's

15

culture. Remember, there are no givens, even though, admittedly, outlaws many times appear attractive. Rather than wasting your precious human resources money on unproductive programs trying to make poor employees better, invest those funds in selection research that targets hiring the right employees. Then your training dollars can be put to good use training the new employees how to raise productivity in your company, for example.

While I advocate betting on cowboys, not horses, I don't include all cowboys. Bet on those in white hats, not on the outlaws. I'm aware that all this sounds a bit depressing. We want to believe that people can change. Traditionally in America, we root for the underdog, and we all love to tell the story about the person who got a second chance and took advantage of it and went on to great successes.

I recall a great lesson I learned from Ted Beers, my boss at PepsiCo. I approached Ted about the possibility of hiring a down-and-out acquaintance of mine from church. This individual had suffered a series of personal misfortunes and had missed a lot of work at three previous jobs, causing his termination at all three of those previous positions. This individual told me he had straightened out his life and was ready to go forth and do good. I was tempted to hire him at PepsiCo. When I explained the situation to Ted, he gave me the following great wisdom which has stood me well over the years. Ted said, "Brooksie, it's nice to know you have this warm human side to you and that you want to try to help this person get ahead in life. When you meet someone like this, it's okay to be compassionate and sympathetic. Take them to lunch, buy their dinner, but don't hire them." Ted was right; people don't change.

Q. If you hire a clod and train him or her, what do you have?
A. A trained clod.

Selection is paramount. It's the most important personnel hiring task carried out by your human resource managers in conjunction with line managers. While we will discuss biographical criterion validity in detail in chapter five, it is imperative to realize the importance of past behavior in predicting the odds of future success.

As illustrated by numerous research studies, past behavior can successfully be used as a guide in predicting future behavior and the chance of success for a given employee applicant, if the proper questions are asked and correctly interpreted. In most cases, existing poor character factors and past behavior can predict future failure. The past is the best predictor of the future.

However, unless you plan to operate your business on divine intervention, you'd better develop a fail-safe employee selection program and leave significant character changes to God and Federal Government social agencies with their CETA and other programs. You can't change the stripes on a tiger or make a silk purse from a sow's ear. People want to believe in change. Otherwise, why would we make New Year's resolutions? But it's important to remember the cold, hard fact that for us mortal humans, birth is easier than resurrection.

As illustrated by the CETA example, all of us have, at some time in our career, been burned by trying to hire with our heart instead of using our head. More often than not, if the employee's personal problems interfered with his or her performance on a former job, they will negatively impact that employee's performance in the position you have to offer. On top of that, there can be a ripple affect, causing disruption among your other employees and their job performance.

The past is the best predictor of the future. Dag Hammarskjöld, former UN leader, said, "Those who don't know history are doomed to repeat it." This holds true in the art of employee selection as well as history. America's top companies know and understand this. We work with them to hire the best employees for the job: those with the best odds of succeeding in their unique corporate environment.

There's an acronym in computer lingo that also aptly applies to the world of employee selection. It's GIGO, meaning garbage in, garbage out. Keep GIGO firmly in mind when you analyze your firm's employee success factors and craft your employee selection process. All of this leads up to the two and only two selection procedures which work in helping to determine past behavior and characteristics vital to employee success. These are the structured job interview and the biographical validity survey. In future chapters we will discuss the structured interview and the biographical criterion validity study and how they can be used in conjunction with a computer to improve your firm's employee selection process.

B.J. and Bubba
Cowboy Tips on Employee Selection

A man who was born to drown will drown on a desert.

CHAPTER THREE

MATCHING JOBS AND PEOPLE

"The person who knows the least repeats it the most."
Chet Buck, Jr., Wyoming Cowboy

Finding the right cowboy for the job does not happen without a lot of careful thought and planning. While I do believe there is a job for everyone, there are a number of key factors that come into play when trying to match people with jobs.

To be sure, the current economic environment and work force availability represent major determinants in your firm's ability to successfully fill open positions with qualified people. While you may not have any control over the economic situation in which your firm operates, you must remain aware of the constantly changing applicant scene.

Yes, things are changing. The significance of change is that the characteristics associated with good hiring at one time may be different at another period of time. Employee selection criteria has always been a fluid process. There has never been, is not, nor will there ever be a magic formula which can predict success all of the time, though many people mistakenly believe that there is. A formula does exist, but it is always changing. Therefore, you must design a system which reflects these changes. For example, high school graduates in one economic period might do just fine, but in another, college education might be associated with success. I frequently run into companies who have been using some type of testing instrument. I always ask, "How satisfied are you with the instrument?" In most cases, they haven't even undertaken a study to determine if the tool is working. Those companies that have conducted a study say, "Well, we checked it out five years ago, and it seemed to be working okay." The key question is, "How is it working today?" Are you convinced that the selection criteria five years ago is the same as today? A 1987 study undertaken by the Institute of Manpower Studies found that fewer than half of those surveyed believed that they were well enough informed about the projected shortage of younger workers, a significant portion of whom make up the front ranks of the bottom half of the organization. In fact, the study revealed that those surveyed were even less informed than they thought they were.

Even as companies are experiencing an abundance of applicants in the wake of the current recession, recruiting obstacles lie ahead. Key elements that comprise work force challenges of the 1990s and beyond include labor shortages, specific skill shortages, and shifts in the work force age, as well as changes in the sex and ethnic diversity of the labor force.

The good news is that in today's economy, people are available. This means that good selection systems, standardized and validated, can work to maximum efficiency. This is in contrast with situations that I faced in the seventies and eighties when people would say, "Brooksie, I think your system is good, but we don't have enough applicants for our jobs." We do have plenty of applicants for our jobs today, and for the foreseeable future this trend will continue. Now is the time for companies to upgrade their work forces, to understand what's going on, and to develop a selection system that matches people with their jobs.

As competition continues to rev up for higher quality goods and services in response to consumer demand, the buyer's market for certain skilled positions will turn into a seller's market. In other words, companies will have to work harder and more intelligently to attract the right people in the numbers required to meet optimum staffing needs.

Companies should be taking a long hard look at their future employee needs and the internal success factors that translate into productive, long-term employees. Firms will need to be more objective and honest about their corporate culture when looking for qualified employees. Instead of concentrating on trying to market their company to prospective employees, they should focus on finding a mesh among the job position, the corporate culture, and the applicant.

Typically, when people problems exist within a company, top managers make one of two assumptions, leading to radically different courses of action. They either assume that something is wrong with the organization or they assume that they are attracting the wrong people.

Under the first and more common assumption, management attempts to change the organization to make it more attractive to prospective employees. The assumption is that there is something wrong with us, that we are an unsuitable mate and must change to make ourselves more attractive to employees. This involves a range of actions such as changing the pay or the benefits, or even tackling the monster of changing the corporate culture itself. Frequently, managers want to train the supervisors to be better managers. Remember, if you don't have the right supervisors, all the training in the world will not make them good managers. From Mr. Thompson's story (See the case study at the end of the chapter.) I learned that regardless of how bad an organization is, how low the pay is, how poor the working environment is, and how bad the supervisors are, there are some people who thrive and do well in that environment. The trick is to learn what is unique about those people. Why are they surviving in a horrible environment? That knowledge can lead to great enlightenment in an organization. This does not mean that organizations should never make attempts to change, but if you don't have the right people in the first place, change is doomed to failure. You're a better person than I am if you can transform a Theory X management style to a Theory Y management style without encountering major disruptions in company morale and productivity.

Unless you are a glutton for punishment, I strongly suggest taking a second alternative: hire a different kind of employee. Under the first scenario, the assumption is that something is wrong with us. Under the second scenario, the assumption is that something is wrong with those people we hire (in light of our corporate culture). It is far easier to change the focus of your employee search than to change the whole organization.

Even if you were to succeed in changing the organization, you would still be faced with the task of finding potential job applicants who would thrive under your new corporate culture and its related success factors. The critical fact would remain the same. You still need to avoid trying to fit the square peg into the round hole; it does not work.

There's a place for everybody in the work environment. We are not all cut out to be rocket scientists. As an example, I remember a study I conducted for a well-known purveyor of fast food in over 200 malls. The company had been focusing its hiring on the academic top ten percent of high school students. My results indicated that these people were five times more likely to quit the job in the first ninety days than were the students in the bottom ten percent. Furthermore, students who were not involved in outside school activities were much more likely to still be on the payroll after one year. While we are betting on cowboys, it is appropriate to remember that we need a few good hands to keep the business running properly.

In order to gain the right perspective on who to hire for open positions, it is first necessary to understand the nature of job satisfaction. Job satisfaction is derived from the worker's positive experience on the job in relation to his or her own set of values. While job satisfaction alone cannot be satisfactorily correlated with high productivity, job dissatisfaction can lead to overt behavior such as absenteeism, tardiness, grievances, and turnover, which are detrimental to the company's success. Other factors, such as supervision, labor market conditions, the person's ability to control or suppress emotions, and interaction with other workers, contribute to the complexity of the work situation.

In large measure, the popular perception of today's worker and work stems from the portrayal of Charlie Chaplin as a helpless cog caught in the machinery of an industrial age. In other words, modern jobs tend to be perceived as repetitive and unchallenging.

On the surface, this would appear to be a rational conclusion. On the other hand, extensive research paints a different picture. As early as 1924, P. S. Florence in *Economics of Fatigue and Unrest and the Efficiency of Labor in the English and American Industry* (Henry Holt & Company, New York, 1924) discovered that jobs that appeared extremely repetitious were not always considered monotonous by workers.

What one person finds monotonous, another worker finds challenging. In an article which appeared in *Journal of Applied Psychology* (Vol. 39, No. 5, 1955, pp. 322-29) titled "The Prediction of Individual Differences in Susceptibility to Industrial Monotony", Patricia Cain Smith stated that to a great extent monotony is dependent upon the individual worker's perception of his or her job. According to Smith, a worker's view of what is repetitive or monotonous differs from a teacher's or researcher's. The latter must take the worker's job perception into account. For the worker, repetition depends upon what he or she perceives in the specific task. Typing is repetitive work in that the fingers are constantly creating keystrokes. However, an adept typist may consider it challenging to create a document without errors. Similarly, a pleasant work environment in the form of an amicable typing pool would go a long way toward alleviating feelings of boredom.

The worker can also perceive job variety in the minute changes of detail as well as in the social situation surrounding the task. Smith concluded that repetition defined as externally observable frequency of occurrence cannot be stated as a valid cause for monotony. Repetition is but one characteristic of many forming the task as perceived by the worker.

Smith's research delved into which characteristics of our individual might predispose him or her to boredom or monotony. The research took place at a small knitwear firm in northern Pennsylvania. The study focused on a group of seventy-two women workers engaged in light, repetitive work. In agreement with previous research, Smith found that such indirect indicators of boredom such as talking, frequency of rest pauses, average working speed, and the shape and variability of the output curve proved to be both unreliable and invalid predictors. Written questionnaires asked such questions as "Do you often get bored with your work?" and "Would you like to change from one type of work to another from time to time?" The frequencies of similar answers to each question were compared by the chi-square method for the entire group under study, and a weighted criterion score devised.

Seven hypotheses were tested with three tenable predictors for employees being susceptible to boredom. The hypotheses that were not supported by the study were that the susceptible worker is more ambitious, tends not to daydream, is extroverted, and is more intelligent.

The three hypotheses that proved successful in predicting susceptibility to boredom in this study were that the worker is more likely to be young, to be restless in his or her daily habits and leisure-time activities, and to be less satisfied with personal, home, and work situation in aspects not directly connected with uniformity or repetitiveness.

In conclusion, Smith offered an eighth hypothesis: that feelings of boredom and monotony are not merely a function of the task performed, but are related to more general factors in the makeup of an individual worker. In contrast to the claims of popular literature, Smith's study described the worker satisfied with performing repetitive work as one content with the existing state of affairs. The worker's satisfaction stems from acceptance of reality instead of arising from stupidity or insensitivity. Smith stated that since the preference for uniformity in work (repetition) relates more to the daily habits of employees outside of the work situation, to the lack of conflict or rebellion in the home, and to contentment both in the factory and out, feelings of boredom or monotony seem to be more symptomatic of other discontent and restlessness than specific to any particular task.

Smith's conclusions have remained stable over the years. The implications are enormous to organizations who wish to improve their front-line hiring. There is no such thing as a boring job, though there are people who do not adapt well to repetitive jobs. This being the case, it is easier and more productive to understand the nature of your jobs and the characteristics of people who perform well in them than it is to change the nature of your organization and its jobs. It cannot be stated too strongly; you must match the right person with the right job.

To explain how front-line selection works at most companies, I developed a concept of hiring I refer to as the Three Sigma Theory (Figure 3-1). To be honest, there is no research to confirm this theory, but I like the way three sigma sounds. Besides, I think when I refer to the Three Sigma Theory I developed, most of my colleagues at the University are impressed. The Three Sigma Theory was developed entirely out of my observations of and hunches about what really happens in the front-line selection process.

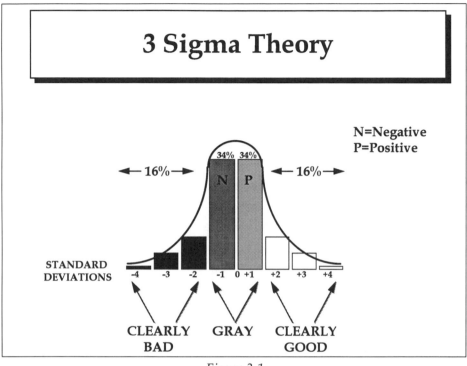

Figure 3-1

Note in Figure 3-1 that a company's applicant pool is represented by a bell-shaped curve. This curve represents what is sometimes called the normal distribution. In the normal distribution, a percentage of good applicants fall in the one to three sigma (hence the name Three Sigma Theory) range on the right side of the curve. This could represent as much as sixteen percent of your applicant pool. These applicants are clearly good. Usually this is known because someone in the organization has worked with them before in a similar job. They are known applicants. Hire them. You don't need a test or a selection procedure if you are fortunate enough to have sufficient job applicants in this range of the curve.

On the other hand, an equal percentage of bad applicants appear on the negative side of the curve. You wouldn't hire them if they scored the highest possible score on any test or selection process. They smell bad, have two heads, or they parked in your private parking space. So, unless they are a blood relative to your boss, there is no need to test. Don't hire them.

An examination of the curve will reveal that most (sixty-eight percent) of your applicants will be in the middle. Thirty-four percent of them will be bad and thirty-four percent will be good. It's a simple concept, but the -1 sigma and the +1 sigma employees are not so easy to distinguish from one another. And, as mentioned in chapter one, the only two proven processes you can use to separate the wheat from the chaff are the structured job interview and the biographical criterion validity study (BCVS).

My own initiation by fire in finding the right people for the job started when I was a personnel manager for the PepsiCo Transportation Division. I learned about employee selection from a very unusual source, and, like much of my real learning, it came the hard way. The message stuck and has impacted my efforts in the employee selection field to this very day. Here's what happened.

I worked for PepsiCo's National Trailer Convoy (NTC), which moved trailer homes from factories to dealer lots. (Don't ask me what moving trailer homes has to do with soft drinks; that's another story.) Our division was run by Mr. Wayne Thompson (I still can't force myself to call him Wayne; it's Mr., if you know what I mean), a battle-scarred veteran of King-of-the-Mountain battles in one of the toughest businesses in America. Mr. Thompson did not like staff managers in general and personnel whippersnappers specifically. But I didn't let that dampen my enthusiasm. I wanted to show him that I was a professional, someone he could rely on.

My opportunity to prove myself came when Mr. Thompson's secretary called me three weeks ahead for an appointment at 2:28 P.M. I knew the odd meeting time and long advance notice were among his intimidation techniques, so I was determined not to let them bother me. Grapevine rumors made it apparent that Mr. Thompson was unhappy with the recruiting and staffing efforts of my department since we took over this responsibility for NTC.

Hiring and keeping people for NTC proved to be a challenge. One particular job only paid $1.60 per hour and required continual calculation without the benefit of adding machines in a room without air conditioning. Promotion opportunities were nonexistent and Theory X supervisors prevailed. More often than not, our employees crossed the street to Minihoma Insurance, which offered clerical jobs in an air-conditioned office with adding machines and paid $2.25 an hour.

I conducted a professional wage and benefit survey confirming the dismal working conditions and rock bottom pay scale at NTC. I was well prepared to give my presentation and escort Mr. Thompson and NTC into the twentieth century.

My heart quickened as Mr. Thompson looked with interest at my slick graphs and quartile charts. I had finally gained his confidence. My God, he had even asked for my recommendations. I offered my professional opinion that we needed to raise our wage from $1.60 per hour to $2.30 per hour. Furthermore, we needed to assign a desk to each clerk, install air conditioning, and purchase electronic calculators to attract qualified employees. Most importantly, I recommended that we train our supervisors in modern management techniques.

"That, sir, would enable me to recruit, hire, and retain qualified clerks for NTC," I concluded. I proudly envisioned Mr. Thompson rising to applaud my presentation.

It didn't happen that way. Mr. Thompson pulled a yellow pencil stub from behind his ear and made a few calculations on the tattered desk pad in front of him. (Mr. Thompson didn't use one of those newfangled calculators either.) He turned to Arnold McCraw, his trusted right hand in all matters of accounting, finance, public relations, and personnel. Arnold wore the green eye shade and plastic pocket protector of his bookkeeping trade proudly. He was Boss Hogg in the flesh.

"Arnold," Mr. Thompson drawled in a deliberate and cynical country accent, "Mr. Mitchell, who I believe is a college-educated boy, says he can hire and keep the help if we spend what I calculate to be 750,000 bucks a year."

The words "college-educated BOY" slammed into me like a Mack truck. I knew I was in deep kaw kaw. My college education taught me that much. Beads of sweat formed instantly on my upper lip.

Mr. Thompson paused for a minute to savor my obvious pain. Then he asked Arnold, "Do we have anybody working for NTC who has been here for more than five years, who is doing a good job in spite of our supervisors, and who is working for minimum wage?"

"You betcha, Mr. Thompson. There's Iola Fay Welch, Prissy Stroop, Ella Jo Miller, Mable Grace Apple, Lydia Lou Landry, and many more."

"Now, Mr. College Boy, don't you tell me we have to spend $750,000 to hire and keep good help. Your job is to find and hire more folks like Iola Faye and Mable Grace."

I saw myself as the young warrior who had challenged the chief and lost. My destiny lay in riding alone in the badlands of ignorant managers for the rest of my career. Then, at the bottom of my despair, I came to a stunning conclusion. Mr. Thompson was absolutely right. He had hit the nail right on the head. Much of his logic was askew, but in terms of hiring practices, he was right. I didn't endorse his sweat shop management practices, but no matter how bad the working conditions, pay, or supervision, there were still, for whatever strange reasons, long-term employees who remained on the job and performed. The key was to determine what was unique about these people and differentiate them from their short-tenured, unproductive counterparts. As soon as I correctly profiled the successful employee, in terms of NTC's viewpoint, our turnover began to decline.

I don't think I ever did gain Mr. Thompson's total respect, but once he did say "Hi, Brooks" when our paths crossed in the executive commode. What more could a college boy ask for?

I continue to treasure the great lesson I learned from Mr. Thompson. It is far easier to change the kind of people you hire than it is to change the organization in which they work. Thank you, Wayne; I mean, Mr. Thompson.

With such an auspicious beginning, it's no wonder I dove head first into the endeavor of perfecting employee selection techniques using revolutionary technology. It was the experience of Mr. Thompson that initiated my search for a solution to the dilemma of matching people and jobs and produced the subject of my doctoral dissertation.

As mentioned earlier, the bottom half of the organization presents some unique challenges. It carries a bulk of the firm's day-to-day work load. Accordingly, the front line represents the last frontier for earning significant productivity gains.

In some cases, matching people and jobs is as simple as learning to differentiate between potential employees who will stay with the company as productive members of the organization and those who will not. It does your firm no good to hire 'good people' this year only to see them leave your employ six months to a year down the road. Likewise, it's foolish to hire 'bodies' that won't grow in experience and productivity. Remember, the same experience for twenty years does not equate to twenty years of experience.

The real task lies not in changing your organization, policies, pay and benefit schedules, or corporate culture but in seeking out and hiring the right people for the positions you have now in your present organization.

Remember, birth is easier than resurrection. While some organizational changes may be helpful, it will be more productive to improve your front-line work force by concentrating your efforts on improving the quality of your available work pool. Hiring the right employees will yield faster and more lasting results than will attempts at organizational and job changes. You can't expect to find good employees if you are looking among the wrong candidates.

B.J. and Bubba
Cowboy Tips on Employee Selection

Every jackass thinks he has horse sense

CHAPTER FOUR
IMPORTANCE OF FRONT-LINE EMPLOYEES

"It ain't how you coach, it's who gets on the bus with you."

Del Wight, Wyoming Cowboy
Defensive Football Coach
San Diego State University

Why are front-line employees important to an organization? There's a simple answer. Front-line employees do the bulk of the day-to-day work and make a big difference in the level of success your company enjoys.

Almost any manager would voice agreement with this conclusion, yet the consensus that people can make the difference between corporate success and failure emerges as a relatively new concept in American labor history.

Prior to 1920, and in many companies still today, front-line employees ranked no higher in importance than a piece of equipment. Likewise, they received similar treatment. If an assembly-line machine broke down, management either fixed it or replaced it. If a hired hand didn't do the job required, he or she was dismissed, another cog in the production wheel was hired. An unlimited supply of labor from the hiring hall kept a steady stream of job applicants flowing to the factories and offices.

I'm not condemning the management practices of those days, although companies managing in that manner today need a few lessons in modern management practices. It was simply a fact of industrial life; people represented a readily available, dispensable asset.

Two landmark events changed management's thinking about employees forever. The Hawthorne Studies and the Scanlon Plan forced companies to rethink their approach to productivity and employees. The conclusions reached and documented by these two events overwhelmingly supported the fact that front-line employees can make a big difference in the success or failure of a company.

The Hawthorne Studies and Scanlon Plan sent a clear warning shot toward the corporate target. If managers didn't pay attention to their people, they risked operating and productivity results hazardous to corporate profits and even to the survival of the firm itself.

The earliest and best known of these two studies in employee motivation and productivity took place at Western Electric Company's Hawthorne Works in Chicago, hence the name, Hawthorne Studies. Originally designed to increase worker productivity through improved lighting, the Hawthorne experiment stumbled upon some interesting conclusions which altered the way management viewed front-line employees.

Conducted in the 1920s, the Hawthorne Studies found that productivity did indeed increase when the electric bulbs were changed. While this was expected, the other findings of the study proved to be even more enlightening. Not only did productivity increase when bulbs were changed to ones with higher illumination values, it also rose when the bulbs were replaced with other bulbs of the original intensity. Furthermore, the Hawthorne experiment also found that workers maintained their productivity levels despite the replacement of bulbs with ones of lower intensity, which substantially lowered the illumination level.

The point was that it didn't matter whether management increased or decreased lighting; either way productivity increased. These results prompted other research studies, which eventually concluded that employee motivation and productivity were linked to employee attitudes. In other words, the attention given to the workers contributed to the changes in productivity, not the fact that the illumination level improved. Wow!

Out of the Hawthorne Studies emerged the concept that team building, even informal teams, helped workers shed the image that they were just pairs of hired hands, stripped of dignity and the desire to contribute more to the corporate effort. Allowing workers to be important provided the incentive to achieve more than expected, giving rise to higher productivity levels.

Much later, Joseph Scanlon of the Massachusetts Institute of Technology took employee involvement one step further. Under the Scanlon Plan, management and worker interests merged in order to achieve higher productivity. This was accomplished through two steps. First of all, workers participated with management to develop new methods to improve productivity and quality levels. Second, rewards for the improved efficiency were distributed to worker teams rather than to single individuals.

The team approach eliminated the possibility of a worker becoming ostracized by his or her fellow employees since the fruits of higher productivity were distributed to the team as a whole. Worker/management committees brought the hired hand into the midst of the work planning process. It allowed workers to buy-in, making increased productivity levels a direct contributor to the employees' own financial well-being, as well as improving their feelings of self worth.

At Texas Instruments we had a program similar to the Scanlon Plan called Work Simplification. This was the direct result of the early pioneering work of Frank and Lillian Gilbroth and Allen Mogensen. I directed the efforts of this program for approximately one year back in the mid-sixties. We took assembly-line operators off the line to ask them for their ideas about how to improve the work. The results were astounding.

One particular example I recall revolved around the wafer-sort operation. This was a job that involved several hundred operators. It was considered to be the worst job available, and was the equivalent of being sent down the river. This job was very tedious, and required operators to look through microscopes for eight hours a day to sort out tiny pieces of colored silicone with a hypodermic suction needle. These colored pieces were put into little Mums jars and the operators kept count of how many chips they sorted with a foot peddle counter. Imagine row upon row of operators with their eyes glued to microscopes sorting tiny silicone chips and keeping track of the count with their feet.

I was involved with bringing these operators into a work simplification meeting and asking how this job could be done better. Immediately one operator suggested using bigger dishes to minimize the chance of missing the dish. What a great idea! We implemented this concept and realized an immediate increase in productivity and quality.

At another meeting one woman noted that she had seen a TV show where a scale was so sensitive that it could actually weigh the ink required to sign a person's signature. She wondered if they could use scales to weigh the chips instead of counting them with their feet. It made a lot of sense to me and other supervisors; however, some engineers were skeptical because they were afraid that operators might overload the scales with bogus silicone chips to increase their productivity. This would be a problem for customers who would then see a significantly higher number of bad chips in their orders. These chips were worth from ten to fifty dollars each, and thousands of them would fit into a small jar. In spite of the engineers' protest, we were able to determine the average weight of a chip, and when the operators no longer had to use their feet to push the peddle, productivity went up by twenty percent.

Most amazing, however, was not the twenty percent productivity increase. When a detailed counting was made to determine the accuracy of the scales, we found that operators had consistently been under reporting the number of chips they had been counting with their feet. Rather than be accused of sandbagging the count (which would be very difficult to measure) they would under report. While the under reporting was noble on their part, it resulted in a significant loss of sales. For example, a Mums jar sold to a customer with 1,000 chips at ten dollars apiece for $10,000 might actually contain 1100 chips. This would be a net loss of $1,000. Needless to say, the use of scales became standard operating procedure at Texas Instruments.

As in any successful corporate plan, management commitment must be clearly exhibited to achieve the desired results. In order to work, the Scanlon Plan or any other productivity improvement program needs complete cooperation and trust between management and worker ranks. While a number of Scanlon Plan formats have evolved over the years, the underlying premise still holds. Front-line employees can make a significant contribution to achieving the goals of management. In other words, management had to be on alert: Failure to pay attention to your people will be hazardous to your profits and may even result in your company's failure.

As discussed in earlier chapters, people don't change very much and a job exists somewhere for almost everyone. The real trick lies in picking the right people for the right jobs. Or, put another way, hiring front-line people who possess the maximum propensity to respond to an enlightened management that desires to capitalize on the conclusions reached by the Hawthorne Studies and the Scanlon Plan remains a key challenge for the management of the twenty-first century.

When I first began the search to discover the secret of hiring successful front-line employees for an organization, it was like a quest for the Holy Grail. A few landmark studies existed, but a lack of practical and significant research compounded the difficulty of finding a solution to the employee selection problem. For the most part, the employment of front-line people was virtually ignored in research and management seminars.

On the surface, I suppose it makes sense. After all, middle and top management jobs are certainly more glamorous and more fun to write about. Additionally, the hefty salaries earned by key personnel and their high corporate profile make it possible to sponsor the research and write books about them. On the other hand, however, in most organizations the number of front-line employees far surpasses that of top management.

Finding, hiring, training, and motivating good worker bees rank as critical objectives for the survival of any organization. Worker bees do the work. They keep the hive producing and the queen fat and happy. Many economists believe that the giant leaps in productivity improvement due to technology are over. We have skimmed the cream. There will be no more slam dunks due to Bessemer furnaces, assembly lines, and automation. Those days are over. This means most future productivity gains will have to be derived from your employees.

The difference between one airline, one store, one hotel, and another stems not from who has the nicest equipment, the prettiest store, or the best rooms, but from who employs the best people. As middle management ranks continue to evaporate, this means those people on the front line of the organization. What a surprise!

Since the days of the Hawthorne Studies, companies have been publicly professing the importance of people to the success of the organization. It represents a great public relations ploy and reads well in the press, but the actions of management speak louder than the words given to employee importance.

Worker bees represent another line of the corporate balance sheet and receive the same deference as a piece of equipment that gets depreciated and replaced as required. But in today's competitive business environment, survival strategies require that the rubber meet the road and that management walk the talk.

We have come full circle back to the real importance of people. Unless a company learns how to locate, hire, and train the right workers, it will find itself at a severe disadvantage as we move through the highly global, competitive nineties.

There is some good news for managers who wish to improve the quality of their worker bees. You cannot pick up a newspaper or business magazine without noticing the tremendous change taking place in the labor force. There's a major and permanent work force revolution in process, and it is reflected in the unusual economic phenomenon of an expanding economy devoid of a corresponding increase in employment. Weekly Fortune 500 companies lay off people by the hundreds of thousands with no plans of ever replacing them.

In fact, the Fortune 500 companies have not contributed to job expansion in the American economy for several years. Furthermore, in 1992 the Labor Department reported that first-time jobless claims soared to all-time record levels. Industry after industry has commenced to trim up and shed the fat gained when foreign competition was an oxymoron. Bill Gates, President of Microsoft, Inc., captures the employee and competitive crisis facing modern management with "Today's companies can no longer afford the luxury of solving their problems with 'masses of asses'."

The significance to companies that have vacancies is that there now exist plenty of good, qualified people anxious to do the work. It hasn't always been this way. In the early eighties I visited companies to discuss the importance of hiring good employees and got a sympathetic but deaf ear. A typical response was: "Brooksie, you don't understand the problem. While we agree with your concepts and believe your employment methods would help us, we don't have any applicants. Nobody is applying for our jobs." My goodness, how the situation has changed in just a few short years.

Now those same managers say, "Brooksie, we don't know what to do. If we place a help-wanted ad in the paper, hundreds of people show up at our door the next morning seeking employment and we need help in screening these people to find the ones best suited for our work."

The most frustrating part of this phenomenon comes not from the extra amount of work required to screen large numbers of applicants, but from the knowledge that somewhere in that mass of applicants there are a few good ones. The fear of choosing the wrong person with the full awareness that the right person is right there, readily available, causes this frustration.

Psychologists refer to this decision dilemma as 'approach-approach,' in which several alternatives exist. Previously, a bad hiring decision was easier to live with because it allowed an employer to use avoidance-avoidance rationalization. In other words, you rationalized, "Well, this hire was a mistake, but the other applicants looked even worse." Faced with equally unattractive choices, bad hires proved inevitable.

The importance of hiring capable front-line warriors is further exacerbated by the fact that many organizational structures are flattening as they shrink. Tall and formal chain of command organizations are proving to be unwieldy and unable to meet the customer-dictated necessity of adroitness, flexibility, and adaptability. Front-line employees can no longer be patronized as bottom-half drones and given no more responsibility than privates in the military. They are now much closer to the product and customer than is management.

The front-line warrior must be given and must be able to accept the decision-making authority of sergeants, lieutenants, and captains. There are no more majors and colonels, and even the ranks of generals have been thinned out through layoffs and early retirements. Now as never before, companies with able and motivated front lines will prosper and outdistance their competitors who continue to languish while waiting for the Second Coming, the next technological miracle to save and absolve them once again. It ain't likely to happen.

The idea of giving more responsibility to front-line employees may sound new and revolutionary. It isn't. My friend and mentor, Dr. Scott Myers, said all of this several years ago in his book, *Every Employee A Manager*. Myers said companies were going to have to let employees at all levels of the organization plan and control their own work. Managers were going to have to stop impeding the front-line employees with archaic systems, procedures, and insecurities. He was right. Yet while many managers praised Myers and professed to implement his ideas, they were sucked back into the comfort of the 'old ways' by the enticement of prosperity fueled by non-competitive markets and short-term technological gains. In those days, managers could humor writers like Myers.

There are some interesting organized labor implications of Myers' research which are similar to those we've observed as a result of hiring good people. Myers knew that if people are allowed to plan, perform, and control their work, the gulf between management and employees is minimized. In other words, if employees are indeed managers, it eliminates the gulf, or the perceived 'us/them' delineation. If there is no us/them delineation, who would be the target of an organized labor campaign? Myers' work at Texas Instruments in this area proved to be critical. Texas Instruments is one of the few large manufacturing companies in the world without an organized labor representation. We have seen a similar phenomenon in companies that hire the best people and give them opportunity. Very few of the users of the Greentree Computer Interview are represented by organized labor.

Now it is no longer good enough to simply pay lip service, or to profess front-line involvement by simply referring to employees as owners or associates, or by saying we make our associates feel responsible. How about allowing your associates to be responsible? The veneer of using a vocabulary to jump conspicuously on the public relations bandwagon of employee involvement is usually transparent to everybody except management. Good employees were always smarter than that. As one front-line assembly operator expressed on a T-shirt she wore to work, "What you do speaks so loudly, I can't hear what you're saying." The meaning to management is this. Get it loud and clear. If you are going to grow and prosper in the next decade, your front-line employees must lead the way. You have no choice; you must listen and heed prophets like Scott Myers or you will slowly wither, twist, and die.

Good hiring is implicit in the concept of improving the front-line work force. As was stated in a previous chapter, people don't change much, so you have to hire them to respond to your unique work environment. If you want front-line employees who can plan and control their work, you must hire employees who are predisposed to accepting responsibility. If people don't want responsibility, you can't train them to accept it. Birth has always been easier than the single recorded incident of resurrection.

On the other hand, front-line employees who are willing to accept responsibility (and given that opportunity can make things happen) can put a square peg into a round hole. They can move an organization forward in ways that make previous technological gains seem insignificant. That's why in Wyoming the smart ranchers bet on cowboys, not horses. I truly believe in that philosophy. It's the cowboys that make things happen. Horses get lame, fall down, get cantankerous, and don't want to come out of the chute. A good cowboy will get back in the saddle day in and day out and get the job done in spite of the horse. I know the same is true of our employees. Bet on employees, not specifically for what they know, but on what they can accomplish with the proper guidance, latitude, and responsibility. This is an analogy you can take to the bank in terms of improving the quality of your work force in the nineties.

The successful hiring of front-line employees differs significantly from the hiring of managers. They are separate phenomena and require separate strategies for successful implementation. There are three reasons for this: time, numbers, and expense.

First, it takes a lot of time to hire a manager. There are usually multiple interviews, site visits, and reference checks. I think, given the implications of a good or bad decision, it is reasonable to assume that this is time well spent, especially at higher levels in the organization where the effect of a single employment decision can increase exponentially. Even at this level, the hiring decision is right only one out of three times. This dismal hit rate is undoubtedly responsible for a significant portion of management's pessimism when it comes to hiring front-line employees. If we spend weeks hiring a top manager and make a good hire only one-third of the time, how can we expect to do a better job hiring our front-line employees with less time? Good question!

Second, an organization typically hires many more front-line employees than managers. This creates both problems and opportunities. The problems are those associated with hiring on a volume basis. In most organizations, there simply isn't enough time (or willingness) to conduct multiple interviews of ninety or more minutes. The time situation is further complicated by companies with multiple locations, sometimes thousands of miles apart.

The opportunity presented by volume hiring is that numbers present the potential for developing hiring profiles through a company and job-specific criterion validity study. Properly developed and validated, a criterion profile can help a company quickly focus on those front-line job applicants who have the highest probability of success. This can't be done with the majority of management positions because of the small numbers involved and the heterogeneity of the job. The specifics of the criterion validity study are discussed in detail in chapter five.

Third, the selection of front-line employees is significantly different from their management counterparts because of the hiring costs involved. It shouldn't surprise anyone that it costs more to hire a manager than a front-line employee. Granting the importance of the front-line work force, few companies would be willing to pay the same per-hire cost at the front-line level as they do at the management level.

The differences of time, numbers, and money have been largely responsible for a major problem in optimizing front-line hiring.

They have caused many managers to lose hope and to be drawn towards the alluring siren which professes there is a pill that can solve the problem. The thought process is as follows: " I don't have time to spend ninety minutes each to interview twenty-five applicants for the shop jobs. Even if I did, I don't have any reason to believe I would be more successful in my hiring 'hit rate.' Besides, I don't want to spend the money it takes to do all of these things I've been told will help me. What I want is a pill. I want to look at them and be sure they don't have blue marks up and down their arms or two heads, and then I want something to tell me if I should hire them or not."

In other words, managers who are understandably frustrated with the hiring process begin to believe (or want to believe) that there is a simple solution to a complex problem. Paper-and-pencil personality and honesty tests have made a fortune by professing to solve this dilemma. "Use the score provided by this test and you don't have to worry anymore about this problem." It ain't that simple. As will be discussed in later chapters, there are some things that can be done to substantially improve the front-line hiring situation and minimize the associated time, number, and money problems. It still takes work and diligence. There is no tooth fairy and there is no pill. I'm sorry, but that's the way it is.

There are a number of reasons that employee selection for the front line of the organization proves to be less than optimum. First of all, recent economic trends have changed traditional management roles and the relationship between management and lower-level employees. For example, moves toward organization decentralization resulted in the delegation of employee selection tasks to line managers who typically do not like to interview and hire. If they really wanted to spend their valuable time interviewing and hiring employees, they would have chosen careers as human resource managers as opposed to line managers. In other words, today's line managers are being expected to perform employee selection tasks completely outside of their specific career choices and for which they have not received the proper training.

Complicating the situation even more, many managers have given up on the employee selection process. This results in the nuisance interviewing and hiring task being pushed even farther down the chain of command. Downsizing and eliminating layers of middle management positions also work to push hiring decisions onto employees not willing or ready to accept this responsibility.

Likewise, the establishment of quality circles, quality control teams, and other forms of participative management have frequently resulted in recommendations that line managers become more involved in the hiring decision. This is as it should be, but if line managers are to become involved and accountable, they must be given tools that can help them be successful in this vital area. At a minimum, this requires standardization of your front-line employee selection program concomitant with an understanding of key success factors for your company's job-applicant evaluation process.

Second, the wide geographical dispersion of front-line personnel in many large organizations obscures the effectiveness of employee selection techniques and the people who are carrying out those duties. It's relatively simple to track the accountability of one-on-one management hires, but the sheer mass of front-line hires and the mobility of today's work force add dimensions to employee selection that cloud the success, or lack thereof, of your company's employee selection program.

Finally, the biggest problem is that, without a clear set of hiring criteria and employee selection goals established ahead of time, there are no benchmarks against which to compare your success or failure in employee selection. It's very important to think clearly through your employee selection goals and benchmarks. Without a thorough analysis of what you want to accomplish, you could be sending the wrong signals to those personnel charged with the responsibility of hiring new employees.

For example, I recently visited the offices of a large Fortune 500 company. On the wall of the employment manager's office hung a large graph depicting the decreasing time to fill applications. Displayed proudly next to the graph was a note from the company president expressing his appreciation for the employment department's success in cutting the application time from twenty-one days to ten.

I don't know if the change resulted from a more timely

response from job applicants or from more efficient work on the part of the employment department, but both the graph and accompanying note from the president could be sending the wrong message. They might encourage managers to improve the graph at the expense of hiring the wrong person for the job.

Wouldn't it have been much better if the graph indicated the number of employees hired in the past month or year who had achieved certain performance levels, or the decrease in time required to train new employees because of the care taken in the selection procedure? I firmly believe this 'I need somebody now!' phenomenon gets reinforced when top management focuses the managers' own monthly and annual performance reviews on hiring time as opposed to the quality of the people they hire.

Remember, there's no pill, no wand to wave, no quick recipe that eliminates the work and the planning required to improve your efforts and success ratio. Forget about off-the-shelf employee selection programs; they are like off-the-rack suits. They just don't fit properly without alterations specific to your organization.

In order to achieve an improved employee selection program, it is necessary to develop some selection criteria against which success or failure can be measured. This means moving beyond intuition and 'gut feel'. Occasionally, I am asked about the importance of 'gut feel' when it comes to hiring. I usually say, "Sure, I believe in gut feelings, but I think it works best in the chitlins section of a hog slaughterhouse." Unfortunately, far more people believe they have the gift of gut feeling than can actually make the right decisions based on this.

Relying on gut feelings is tantamount to flying by the seat of your pants. Managers who say they hire based on 'gut feel' are usually using that as an excuse for not taking the time to do the job right, either because they don't want to or don't know how to. Besides, if you don't have any valid tracking techniques for benchmarking your employee hiring success, how do you know if you hired the best person for the job or not?

Although management's actions frequently speak louder than words, front-line employees are increasingly important in today's global market, and it is easier to hire them 'right' than it is to change them once you have them on the payroll. The right employees will respond and produce for an organization that genuinely gives them the opportunity to do so.

In following chapters, we are going to look at the structured job interview and the criterion validity study, the only two proven methods that can improve the front-line hiring decision.

B.J. and Bubba
Cowboy Tips on Employee Selection

*A cowboy who straddles a fence
has a sore crotch.*

CHAPTER FIVE

WHAT DOES NOT WORK, WHAT WORKS

"The difference between genius and stupidity is that genius has its limits."

B.J.

Too many American firms use employee selection techniques that simply do not work. Why do companies spend valuable time, money, and effort on human resource programs that do not deliver the goods in terms of hiring the right employees for the right jobs and controlling expensive turnover? Rather than not use any planned or structured employee selection program, human resource managers turn to unproven techniques in search of a comfort factor. The 'I'm using some sort of commercially marketed employee selection process, so I must be doing something right' syndrome can actually do more harm than good.

I think the rise in popularity of employee leasing is a direct result of management's frustration with the front-line hiring process. They know that what they're doing isn't working, so they have some desire to turn this over to an outside company and let them manage their employees. It would be nice if it were that simple. That's equivalent to trying to turn your health over to someone else. It just simply does not work.

Employing ineffective selection techniques has been proven to negatively impact employee turnover rates, causing higher employee costs, and a decline in employee morale. All of this, usually sooner than later, leads to tremendous decreases in quality and increases in the overall cost of producing. The use of improper selection techniques can also work to cause unintentional discrimination problems at your firm. Research has shown that short people receive fewer job offers than tall people. Likewise, deep-seated prejudices of individual interviewers view fat people as lazy and undisciplined. To illustrate how ridiculous personal prejudices can be, one sewing machine company executive believed that stubby fingers inversely related to job performance in a sewing machine operation.

These biases were very evident in a controlled study we conducted for a large American corporation. The same interviewers hired applicants using two techniques. Technique one used their traditional non-structured interviewing, and technique two employed interpreting and hiring based on the results of the computer-assisted interview. This allowed them to judge applicants before actually seeing them. The productivity was greater and turnover was less for the computer-assisted interview (CAI) group. However, the most remarkable conclusion was the lack of bias.

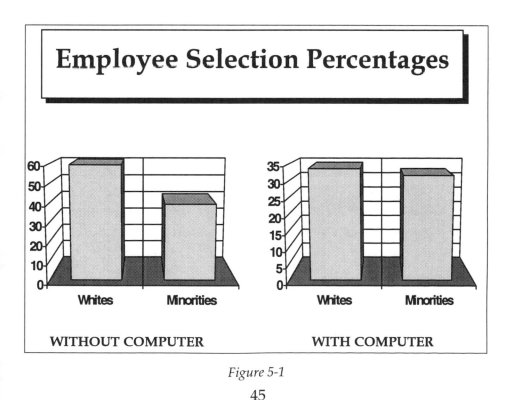

Figure 5-1

Specifically, when interviewers hired traditionally, they showed a significant disparate impact against minorities; yet when they were using the computer interview results, the disparate impact evaporated. Why? Because the CAI provided more objective data. When I presented these results to the interviewers they were shocked. They could not believe that they were prejudiced. Yet, the results belied this.

Intuition and 'gut feel' often prove to be poor barometers for predicting employee success for the majority of managers and interviewers. Don't be tricked into a false sense of security by believing you are one of the chosen with an infallible gift of intuition or 'gut feel' that allows you to navigate around the perils of choosing the wrong employees. Worse yet, don't permit expressions of intuition or 'gut feel' to excuse you or your company from establishing a proven and effective employee selection program.

Numerous studies have consistently reported that trained interviewers, when using unstructured techniques, make up their minds about an applicant within the first three minutes. Personal appearance ranks as the major determining factor in the decision to hire that person during that three-minute decision-making process. The rest of the interview time is then spent confirming the original decision. If it is a negative decision, the interviewer begins working his or her way out of the interview. If it is a positive decision, the interviewer begins doing most of the talking trying to sell the applicant. This is a direct violation of Brooksie's rule of fifty-one percent which says that a job applicant must come at least fifty-one percent of the way. If you have to hard sell then you are diminishing your chances of a successful hire.

While we want our managers to be decisive, I think this is carrying the theme a bit too far, especially in an area as crucial to a firm's success as employee selection. In addition, as noted above, personal prejudices tend to creep into the process causing the firm to miss out on potentially successful employees and possibly leaving the company susceptible to discrimination actions in the future.

Everyone is susceptible to these prejudices, even trained psychiatrists. Dr. John Greist, a pioneer in the area of computer interviewing, conducted research several years ago to investigate manic-depressive patients of trained psychiatrists. He asked the psychiatrists for a few facts about their patients. These were critical factors he derived from a criterion validity methodology. He then asked the psychiatrists to predict whether or not these patients would attempt suicide or in fact commit suicide. Dr. Greist then made a prediction of the suicide attempt rate based on his objective facts. His predictions were three times more accurate than were the psychiatrists who were treating the patients. Why? Because the psychiatrists had become sucked into the trap of becoming overly influenced by the person as opposed to the objective facts.

One classic study clearly illustrates how biases work their way into the employee selection process. In the study, an actor was sent to one hundred trained industrial interviewers. In each case, the actor's visit was preceded by the interviewers receiving a job description and a series of specific questions that they were supposed to ask the applicant. The actor gave the same response to every interviewer. The interviewers were then asked to make a hiring decision based on the assumed job opening.

One year later, the same interviewers were contacted and given the same job description and series of questions to ask the applicant. In this instance, a different actor appeared for the interviews and responded to the same questions in the exact way the first actor did. The interviewers were then asked to make the second hiring decision.

In other words, all factors that entered the decision-making process were the same except for the actor exchange. On the surface, you would expect similar outcomes in terms of a hiring offer. The actual result: actor one received the job offer seventy-five percent of the time while actor two received the job offer only twenty-five percent of the time.

The difference between the two actors consisted of one variable: height. Actor one stood 6'5" while actor two's stature was 5'5". Underlying biases resulted in the taller actor receiving a bonafide job offer at twice the rate as did the shorter actor. Don't be surprised if the same type of biases have crept into your existing employee selection interview process, short-circuiting your company's ability to attract and maintain the best employee base available.

A recent *Harvard Law Review* article found the problem of visual discrimination so pervasive that it recommended placing a screen between the interviewer and the job applicant. The problem of bias in the employment interview has been so overwhelming that one study by Tubiana and Ben-Shakhar (1982) even suggested that the personal interview be completely eliminated and replaced with paper-and-pencil information-gathering techniques. While this might make sense and remove most bias, it is not reasonable to expect that a company is not going to hire a person without having a good look at them first.

The problem of bias has led many companies astray by causing them to search for an objective test score (pill) that would alleviate the necessity for a well-reasoned decision process. A study by J.J. Asher in a 1988 issue of *Personnel Psychology* confirms the relative insignificance of personality/psychological factors in the prediction. His study also found that intelligence and aptitude tests were also weak in their predictive ability.

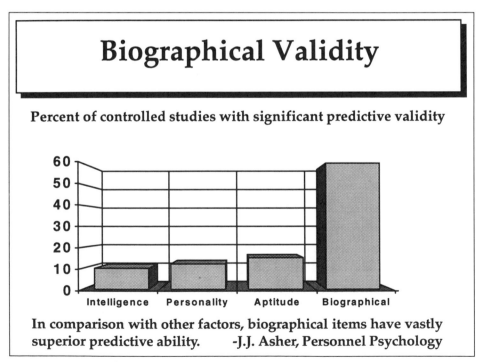

Biographical Validity

Percent of controlled studies with significant predictive validity

Intelligence Personality Aptitude Biographical

In comparison with other factors, biographical items have vastly superior predictive ability.   -J.J. Asher, Personnel Psychology

Figure 5-2

People say to me sometimes, "Isn't intelligence important?" To me, intelligence is like a typing score. That is, after you can type 60 words a minute with three or fewer errors, that's good enough. A secretary who types 120 words a minute is not twice as good as someone who types 60 words a minute. Intelligence tests might effectively screen out the bottom ten or fifteen percent: however, you could probably talk to those applicants and realize that they are not playing with a full deck anyway, so the intelligence test is not that important. As Asher pointed out and as depicted in Figure 5-2, biographical factors do predict. (These will be discussed in detail later.)

Many other interviewer problems work to sabotage the employee selection process. According to Paul Hawkinson, publisher of the recruitment publication *The Fordyce Letter*, initial on-site interview duties are often assigned to new management trainees or middle managers being phased out of the organization. This leads to people making hiring decisions who do not have a good idea of the specific job requirements, or even worse, who don't possess the right attitude to perform a good interviewing and hiring job.

Research also reflects that interviewers spend too little of the interview time learning about the job applicant. Aspen Tree Software's own Pat Engler-Parish, who heads our customer development department, performed research for her Master's degree at the University of Wyoming which confirmed that interviewers talk over eighty percent of the time during a half-hour interview and forty percent of the time talk about themselves. To be sure, not a very good format for learning about the job applicant and his or her potential for success as an employee in the organization.

Information on an applicant gathered in the pre-interview stage can also come into play, affecting the outcome of the interview and subsequent decision to offer a job. Research by Schneider, Hastorf, and Allsworth (1979) found that final judgments can be unduly influenced by initial impressions.

Tucker and Rowe (1979) also investigated first-impression error. Their research consisted of asking seventy-two students to read and evaluate interview transcripts after they examined a letter of reference. Study results indicated that interviewers who first read an unfavorable letter were more likely to give the job applicant less credit for past successes and to hold the applicant more personally accountable for past failures. The research also showed that the decision to hire closely correlated to interviewers' casual interpretations of past successes and/or failures.

Other employee selection techniques that have been proven to provide dismal employee success predictions include psychological and personality testing. Despite the readily available evidence, human resource managers resort to these tests because they believe it is better than doing nothing in trying to screen applicants and narrow the field of potential employees. Don't be too sure.

Psychological and personality tests perhaps do provide some validity and utility when used in conjunction with filling positions for managers and higher level positions; however, for filling slots at the bottom half of the organization, it remains virtually impossible to correlate personality and psychological factors with employee success.

The main attraction for using psychological and personality tests rests in their descriptive ability. The kicker lies in the inability to go from description to accurate prediction. Some of the blind reliance on psychological and personality tests to ferret out the optimum employee almost harkens back to the days of phrenology, the studying of bumps on a person's head to determine character.

Occasionally a test publisher will ask for my endorsement of their personality/psychological test as a pre-employment tool. If I am feeling a bit on the surly side, I will take the time to answer the 100 to 300 questions typically found on such tests. When I am finished, the administrator usually goes through a complicated scoring procedure that may take several minutes of computer time. When he is finished, he will inform me the test describes me as a highly effervescent, creative individual who has a hard time with details and authority. My immediate response is "Bull's-eye, that's me!" This reaction always causes the test salesman to get wild-eyed and excited. "Wow," he says, "Isn't that exciting?" I am sure he thinks my endorsement is imminent.

"Not particularly," I respond. "Now, I have two questions for you. First, why didn't you just ask me what my personality was? Why did I have to answer 300 questions to determine what I would have readily told you if you had just asked me? Second, now that you have described me, predict me! What does it mean in terms of my future job performance?"

The salesman is crestfallen and realizes the dilemma I have presented him. Description does not necessarily mean prediction. It never has. For example, my insurance agent, Bill Skeeters, has consistently been one of the nation's top sales agents. Bill would always be measured as a shy, quiet individual by most personality tests. These are two personality characteristics almost never associated with success as a life insurance sales agent. But I have bought millions of dollars of insurance from Bill because he is one of the most solid individuals I know. He is the man I want on my side if the going ever gets tough. Others buy insurance because of an attraction to a personality different from Bill's. I repeat, description does not equal prediction.

A few years ago I met with a national association of the top life insurance agency managers. I asked the agents to describe some characteristics of their successful agents. They came up with typical personality-type adjectives such as out-going, self-starter, knows lots of people, friendly, effervescent, popular, and etc. I then asked the managers if they could name some successful agents who possessed these characteristics. Of course, they quickly named some agents. Next, I asked them if there were any agents who had the opposite characteristics yet were still successful. The answer was "Yes, but we don't understand that phenomenon." So they chose to ignore it. I rest my case in relation to the difficulty of equating personality description with personality prediction.

Most psychological and personality tests ask hundreds of questions. The supposed rationale behind this is to measure a number of personality dimensions such as aggressiveness, team player characteristics, independence, etc. Assuming that tests can successfully measure these multiple dimensions, a problem still arises from the fact that the hiring decision is a single decision. Therefore, it doesn't matter if you can measure twenty-five characteristics; you still have to make a single hire/no hire decision.

Further complicating the situation, humans, being very adaptable, tend to play their strengths. Thus, a person who is very shy may instill confidence in some people. Likewise, a person with an aggressive personality may intimidate some people. Either personality characteristic can operate successfully in a wide variety of jobs.

What about intelligence? Look at it this way. Consider intelligence in relation to a typing-speed test score. Once you are adept enough at typing to type 60 words a minute, that's enough for most jobs. In the same vein, a person with an I.Q. of 100 or more, more than likely has enough intelligence to perform the vast majority of non-exempt jobs satisfactorily. Therefore, if an intelligence test possesses any value whatsoever, it simply rests in its ability to screen out borderline morons and others not related to top management. It makes more sense to determine this in a very short conversation than to waste valuable time and resources conducting lengthy psychological and personality tests.

Reference checking represents another major area of concern for the company looking to hire new employees. The practice of checking references has always come under suspicion for two very valid reasons. Number one, numerous studies reflect that references tend to be weighted toward the positive. Number two, and becoming more important in today's litigious society, there is a tremendous legal liability coincident with giving a bad reference that might prevent a person from gaining employment.

The above problem areas do not mean that you completely disregard reference checking because you can derive value by verifying employment dates and employment history. On top of that, you could ask references listed on the application form to recommend additional references: ones who may end up being more objective about the applicant or more knowledgeable about that person's work habits and work experience.

Now that we understand what does not work, it is time to turn our attention and your company's resources to employee selection techniques that aid the task of hiring and keeping the right employees for your firm.

At the risk of repeating myself, there is no pill that will solve your employee hiring problems. Employee selection requires a bit of hard work, but more than that, it demands working smarter and using techniques that deliver the goods.

If you are reading this book for a quick-fix solution, stop right now, put it down, and pick up your Sunday comics section. Your chances of finding a quick fix are better by reading Dick Tracy than by reading a serious discussion about effective employee selection techniques. After all, he has access to all the futuristic gadgets right at his fingertips.

If quality people really do make a critical difference between the success or failure of a company, why do managers devote so little attention to developing an effective hiring program and search instead for a magic solution? Do top management seek a pill for their research and development efforts? No, they spend years and countless man-hours and dollars toward perfecting new technologies.

The same philosophy holds true in other corporate functions such as accounting, finance, product development, etc. Does your company make major equipment purchases without analyzing the benefits and drawbacks of the lease versus purchase decision? Do you engage in major plant expansions without considering return on investment or a changing market or economic environment? Of course not! If you do, then you better stop reading this book right now, because you will not be around long enough to implement an employee selection program.

Imagine the lunacy of looking for a pill or short cut to developing a new product. This is typically accomplished only through extensive market research, intensive testing, and follow-up evaluation. According to *New Product Development*, published by Point Publishing Company in Point Pleasant, New Jersey, the grocery products industry alone spent nearly $167 billion to develop and introduce 20,000 new products over a recent ten-year period.

Though no two companies operate alike, corporate product teams strive to define the process and cost of making a product as well as monitoring its potential and progress toward those goals. All of these resources are directed toward achieving a successful new product launching. Put into perspective, the implications of a failed new product may be less than the impact resulting from the deterioration of a firm's work force due to an ineffective employee selection process.

Thus, the development of an effective employee selection program and its implementation should receive no less effort and dedication to its success than that given to other vital corporate functions. Continual attention and hard work, not a quick fix, are the only answers to improving the work force.

Now, I will briefly introduce you to what really does work in the world of employee selection. In effect, there are only two main proven employee selection techniques:

1. The structured employment interview (especially the computer-assisted employment interview), and
2. A company- and job-specific biographical validity study.

Take my word for it, these are the only employee selection items on which you need to concentrate your human resource time and effort to perfect. In fact, you don't have to take my word at all. Extensive controlled research studies clearly demonstrate that these are the only employee selection techniques that will work at the bottom level of the organization.

The following chapters will provide more in-depth discussion of the rationale for and the practical implementation of the biographically anchored criterion validity (BVS) study, the structured employment interview, and the computer-assisted employment interview.

B.J. and Bubba
Cowboy Tips on Employee Selection

*It's easier to rope a hoss than it is
to bust'm.*

54

CHAPTER SIX

THE STRUCTURED EMPLOYMENT INTERVIEW

"A fool kin ask more questions in an hour
than ten savvy people kin answer in a year."

Mike McGill, Wyoming rancher

It is estimated that American companies spend countless billions of dollars annually to replace and retrain workers lost through excessive turnover, and mostly because the wrong employees were hired in the first place. So, how do you find the right employee?

Nobody wants to buy a pig-in-a-poke. Everybody wants to see the horse that they are buying and this holds especially true when hiring a new employee. You want to have a good look at prospective employees before you commit to hiring them. That only makes good business sense. Will Rogers might have never met a man he didn't like, but Will obviously never met some of the characters you have encountered in your hiring process and did not have to depend on any of these fellas or gals to turn out his newspaper columns, roping displays, or Ziegfield Follies shows either.

It is just not reasonable to assume you are going to hire job applicants sight unseen. So if you gotta take a peek, how do you make the most of the interview process? Unfortunately, there is no easy answer—no pill to solve this headache. It takes a lot of hard work and well thought-out effort. For my money, I bank on the structured employment interview.

In fact, based on what I know from both research and practical experience, the structured job interview (when properly administered) is the single most powerful selection tool in existence. I will bet on the opinion of a line manager who has conducted a structured job interview as opposed to any test in the world!

Perhaps your firm already utilizes a series of set questions on your application form with the intention of removing bias from the interview process and gaining key information on the prospective employee. You may say this is a suitable substitute for a structured interview. Besides, you contend that your skilled interviewers know what to look for and how to draw it out during the more relaxed unstructured job interview. Wanna bet?

While I do not expect you to have research studies and reams of documents backing up your misplaced belief, I wager that your claims are backed more by wishful thinking and that venerable 'gut feeling' than on concrete evidence. On the other hand, I will prove beyond the shadow of a doubt that the structured employment interview serves as a key element in a far superior employee selection process.

Sure, the structured employee interview intimidates some people. There is a lot of rationalizing going on for not performing the structured interview. "Our interviewers don't know how to do it properly and it makes them feel uncomfortable," or "Our line managers have to perform the face-to-face interviews and don't like to do human resource functions." Or perhaps the biggest excuse of all, "We don't have time to do it." Do any of these protestations sound familiar?

Pure bunk. Line managers, not human resource managers, should be held responsible for the final hiring decisions. Ultimately they have to live with the employees and their job performance is on the line and, therefore, they should be interested enough to use the best hiring tools available to acquire the right employees.

You don't use outmoded machinery in your industrial operations at the expense of your competitive position in the market place You don't continue to use pens and pencils where personal computers will do the job faster as well as more accurately and efficiently. You don't depend on the mails for fast delivery of important documents when a fax machine can get the job done in minutes. If you do, you can stop reading this book now, because you won't be in the race much longer.

Your line managers would be screaming bloody murder if you did not provide them with the right tools to get the job done right the first time. Therein lies the paradox, the rub, the apparently unsolvable dilemma. How do you convince your line managers to perform the structured employment interview so as to reap the considerable value derived from it?

This goal remains even more challenging given that the reward and accountability system in force at most firms is cast to reinforce other skills and measurements. On top of that, the obvious career choice (self selection) in the field of line management further complicates the transition to tasks where the softer and more subtle human interaction communication skills are required, skills many line managers consider light years away from their day-to-day responsibilities in the trenches.

To sum it up, you have line managers who don't know how to conduct a structured employment interview, don't like interviewing, don't think they have the time to do the interviewing (even though they have the time to search for replacement employees and train them), and are quite positive that the structured employment interview and its related criterion validity study are positively related to witchcraft or else equate their chances of success with winning at the craps table in Las Vegas. For those of you who need this translated in plain English: they don't give a damn about the structured job interview process.

To save face, most line managers profess to have divine intuition or 'gut feel.' A few may even acknowledge their lack of interviewing skills and try abdicating this responsibility to human resource managers.

They express this generosity with great bravado, introspection, and enthusiasm. "I let the pros do the hiring for me and my operation. I have more important things to do with my time. I have an operation to run to keep this business profitable. After all, those HR people have special training for this sort of thing, so why should I pretend to know more than they?"

In order to solve this hiring crisis situation, you must adopt the following set of hiring principles:

A. Employees do make the difference.

B. You can't transform employees so you must hire right.

C. Line managers want to see 'em before they hire 'em.

D. Line managers must assume responsibility in the hiring decision.

E. The only way to improve the hiring decision is to have line managers conduct a structured employment interview.

F. Any empirical scoring of the interview must emanate from a company- and job-specific criterion validity study.

GREAT INTERVIEW QUESTION

How much money do you expect to earn working for our company?

GREAT ANSWER

All of it.

The structured employment interview is a process of methodically and thoroughly asking pre-determined open-ended questions (as opposed to questions which can be answered with a yes or no response) of every serious job candidate. An example of an open-ended question would be, "Betty, tell me how your plans for future education will be affected by your employment with our company." A closed-ended question delving into the same topic area would be, "Betty, are you planning to go to school?"

A properly conducted structured employment interview takes a minimum of sixty to ninety minutes to conduct. To be optimal, the interviewer must ask all of the same open-ended questions of each applicant. The interviewer must refrain from making a decision during the initial stages (the first three minutes) of the interview. It isn't easy and it takes a lot of training to conduct properly. Yet the potential is enormous.

A classic *Journal of Occupational Psychology* (Vol. 61, 1988, pp. 275-290) article by Wiesner and Cronshaw concluded that the structured interview still represents the best and worst employee selection instrument in the employee-hiring universe. The best because of the potential for significant improvement in the employment decision. The worst because it is seldom conducted properly and is subject to old biases.

Wiesner and Cronshaw report the structured interview is far superior to the traditional unstructured interview. They base their conclusion on a meta-analytic investigation of 150 controlled and reported interview studies. Using meta-analytic investigation, a new research technique that has been evolving over the past fifteen years, we don't have to perform new research to test the validity of structured interviewing versus unstructured interviewing. We can review previously proven, controlled studies published in the right, rigorous journals to see if there is a common conclusion. Wiesner and Cronshaw state, "The prediction for a difference by interview structure was strongly supported . . . the unstructured interview proved to have the least validity of all interview types . . . . [I]n fact, the structured interviews had mean validity coefficients twice those of unstructured interviews." Putting it another way, if you use unstructured interviews, you may be leaving fifty percent on the table in terms of your successful hire hit rate.

You may be wondering why I would recommend using the structured employment interview if it has the potential of being one of the worst selection techniques. There's a method to my madness. First of all, let us take a look at the reasons for its bad press. The major reason the structured employment interview fails to produce good results stems from the fact that most interviewers do not know how to use the structured interview effectively. Plain and simple, they have not been properly trained.

Second, since the interviewer is obligated to ask all of the questions in the format, it is probably the most time consuming interview method, enticing people to try shortcuts that don't work.

On the plus side, the survey of over 150 controlled and published studies of employment interview research in the Wiesner and Cronshaw article found the structured employment interview twice as predictive as its unstructured counterpart. Of course, this assumes that critical factors such as interviewer training and length of interview are properly controlled.

Wiesner and Cronshaw advise interview practitioners "to use the structured interview (as opposed to the unstructured interview) wherever possible. The structured interview questions should be based on formal job-analytical information and every attempt should be made to maximize the reliability of the structured interview."

That's where Dr. Brooks Mitchell and Aspen Tree Software fit in. We may live and work in the Wild West but we don't sell quick-fix, cure-all snake oil elixirs or solutions out of the backs of buckboard wagons. We specialize in tailoring proven employee selection techniques to your operations.

The structured employment interview is at the heart of our computer-assisted employment interview programs. The computer asks the same questions of every applicant. In fact, the computer asks the applicant the same questions in the same fashion and never misses a question, thereby maximizing the reliability of the interview and ensuring that personal biases are left outside of the interview process.

According to a recent *Wall Street Journal* article, more and more companies are moving toward the structured employment interview format. These companies are tired of interviewers chit-chatting away valuable corporate time discussing the Colorado Rockies expansion team's prospects or whether or not Da Bulls will repeat as NBA Champs. Even more importantly, the unstructured interview process is failing to hire the best qualified people to keep the companies running efficiently.

If you don't take my word for it, you can use the simple chi-square computing guide in Appendix A of this book to determine if your current selection procedures are working. If this calculation reveals you are using a successful employee selection procedure, don't fix what ain't broke. Keep using it. Better still, call me and I'll include your success story in the next edition of this book.

The Wiesner and Cronshaw study suggested that interview validity stemmed largely from interview reliability. Inherent in the study hypothesis was that certain interviewing types, such as the structured interview, are more reliable and hence more valid. In the study, structured interviews delivered consistently and substantially higher predictive validity coefficients than unstructured interviews.

In an article on the selection interview by Robert E. Carlson, Paul W. Thayer, Eugene C. Mayfield, and Donald A. Peterson in *Personnel Journal* (Vol. 50, No. 4, April 1971, pp. 268-75), the researchers concluded that only the structured interview generated the information that permitted the interviewers to agree with each other on which employee to hire. Under the structured format, the interviewers knew what to ask and how to interpret the data received. In addition, the interviewer in the structured situation never forgot to ask a question and applied the same frame of reference to each applicant, helping to ensure that personal bias was left out of the decision process. In conclusion, the researchers considered the highly structured interview as possessing the greatest potential for valid employee selection.

A study by Robert L. Dipboye reported in the *Academy of Management Review* (Vol. 7, No. 4, 1982, pp. 579-586), points out the dangers of not using a structured interview since interviewers' pre-interview evaluations of applicants tend to be self-fulfilling. This self-fulfilling prophecy plays itself out in a variety of ways, including how the interviewer conducts the interview, how the conduct of the interview impacts the behavior of the interviewee, how the interviewer perceives the interviewee's performance in the interview, and how the interviewer's casual interpretation of the interviewee's performance in the interview confirms the interviewer's pre-interview evaluation of the applicant.

A structured employment interview would help alleviate self-fulfilling prophecies in the hiring process. By sticking to a structured format with pre-designed questions focusing on specific criteria, the interviewer stays clear of 'adjusting' the interview based on preconceived ideas or prejudices.

Now that you are assured that the structured interview is the route to take to successful hiring practices, let us investigate what makes a structured interview. In simple terms, the structured interview asks set questions of every applicant in the same order and in the same manner. That way, no pre-judgment short-circuits the hiring decision-making process. All applicants start on equal footing in their attempt to land a job with your firm. Each applicant is judged on the probability of his/her success in your corporate work environment and not on skin color, height, weight, sex, political beliefs, or love or hate of the Mets.

To be effective, the structured interview must be based on a very detailed job analysis backed by questions and more probing questions. This does not represent earth-shattering knowledge. It is just good ol' common horse sense. If this is the case, then why don't many companies use the structured employment interview process?

One of the main reasons rests in your firm's underlying (both clearly stated and implied) corporate culture. Take an honest look at your reward system. Does it reward managers for hiring good people or does it keep meaningless statistics on hiring times, etc.? Be realistic. This means big bucks to your bottom line and maybe even your ability to keep your job. Did that get your attention? It should.

The reward structure does not say hire quality people. The reward structure says hire bodies. Take a look at your human resources reports. More than likely, you will find figures reporting how many people were hired last month, the average length of an opening, the interview process time, etc. Do you think your human resource people are dummies? They understand the situation real quickly. Round 'em up, get 'em in, come up with a magic number, and then hire 'em. It's a numbers game. At the bottom half of the organization, we find the following deplorable situation: not only does unstructured interviewing occur almost every time but the 'interviewer' rarely invests more than five to ten minutes, max, per applicant.

Let that sink in . . . five to ten minutes, max. How many other critical business decisions do you make after only spending five to ten minutes (with probably half of that time devoted to the weather or sports or whatever) to consider the options? In that short time span, what can the hiring decision be based on? Let me guess . . . appearance, first impressions, and, oh yes, 'gut feel.'

Even the most experienced interviewers take two to three minutes to make up their minds as to whether or not this applicant is a serious contender for the job, not to mention whether or not he or she is the best qualified among all the applicants for the position. What chance do your untrained line managers and less experienced staff managers have to make the right hiring call within that limited time frame? That leads us back into the vicious circle of the unstructured interview where you routinely leave fifty percent on the table. Without a doubt, the structured employment interview can improve your hiring operations by delivering qualified people who will not be leaving your firm within months after being hired.

There are costs involved with establishing an effective structured employment interview program. First of all, you have to invest company resources (time, effort and money) to develop the proper success criteria. This involves analyzing your unique corporate culture, the specific job requirements, etc., in order to develop the appropriate application and follow-up in-person interview questions.

Then there is the time it takes to conduct the actual face-to-face structured interview. Roughly, that will consume at least sixty to ninety minutes to cover all the bases required in the structured interview process.

I can hear you saying, "Brooksie, we just cannot do that. We cannot tie up our people for that long doing those sorts of things."

You are faced with a real Catch 22. You cannot afford to tie up your operation's line people. You say you know structured interviewing is good in theory and probably good even in practical situations, but in the real world of competitive corporate life, it rarely gets accomplished at the bottom half of the organization. Besides, you protest, it's a real boring process. Consequently, a great deal of potential improvement in the hiring process never gets realized.

Well, Aspen Tree Software and I are here to help you break out of that vicious cycle with implementation of the structured employment interview. A substantial amount of empirical research clearly proves its ability to significantly improve the odds of hiring the right people. More importantly, my years of practical experience helping top American companies improve their employee selection functions have paid big dividends in lower turnover rates and reduced overhead and operating costs.

As will be explained in detail later in this book, my partial solution to the structured interview dilemma has been to develop a computer-assisted version of this process. The computer-aided interview was implemented at a large division of First Data Corporation, a division of American Express. To test the system, First Data Corporation instructed their interviewers to hire one group of applicants by using traditional (unstructured) methodology, and to hire another group by using the structured interview guide provided by a computer-assisted employment interview. The results (Figure 6-1) were dramatic in terms of the increased retention rate for the group hired as a result of a structured interview.

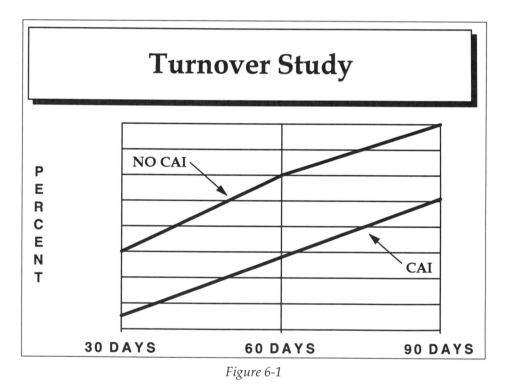

Figure 6-1

Even I was surprised by the dramatic differences in the two groups. But why should I have been? As the Wiesner and Cronshaw study indicated, structured interviewing can improve the hit rate by up to fifty percent. This certainly was the case at First Data Corporation.

The computer interview is a tool, not a pill. I don't have any pill to offer. To achieve these improvements and cost savings, you need to commit to putting forth the necessary effort and resources. It is a simple and clear-cut choice. Either reposition your company in the competitive global marketplace or stick with your present employee selection practices and spend your firm's valuable and limited capital money and people resources to continually hire and train people to replace those leaving the company.

You do not want to hire the best mule out of a pack of losers; you want to run with the best horse available.

**B.J. and Bubba
Cowboy Tips on Employee Selection**

He may be the fastest mule in Wyoming, but he still ain't gonna win the Kentucky Derby.

CHAPTER SEVEN

THE BIOGRAPHICAL CRITERION VALIDITY STUDY

"A cowboy who confesses to small faults
hopes you will think he has no big ones."

By far the best test for uncovering quality, down-to-earth, honest, hard-working people harkens back to the 1930s. At the time, Gene Autry ranked as the number one cowboy star in the world and a real honest-to-goodness hero, when there still was such a thing. Befitting his image, Autry devised a list of do's and don'ts to illustrate exemplary citizenship. This Wrangler's Ten Commandments, so to speak, provided the proper direction for young children the world over.

Gene put forth his convictions in what he termed "The Cowboy Code."

THE COWBOY CODE

- A cowboy must never shoot first at a smaller man or take unfair advantage.
- He must never go back on his word or a trust confided in him.
- He must always tell the truth.
- He must be gentle with children, the elderly, and animals.
- He must not advocate or possess radically or religiously intolerant ideas.
- He must help people in distress.
- He must be a good worker.
- He must keep himself clean in thought, speech, actions, and personal habits.

- He must respect women, parents, and his nation's laws.
- A cowboy is a patriot.

To date, I have yet to unearth a better measure of a man or woman. In a perfect world, it would be easy to find people who could pass the test of "The Cowboy Code." However, in the imperfect business world we exist in, we must devise other methods to ferret out qualified employees.

That's where the Biographically-Anchored Criterion Validity Study (BCVS) enters the picture. It is one of the oldest and most validated selection procedures around. The BCVS is a statistical procedure for determining the empirical probability of a person achieving a certain criterion. It derives from a series of scores which predict the probabilities of specific outcomes such as performance, tenure, sales results, absenteeism, or other employee characteristics which can be specifically measured.

Just what is a biographical item? Simply stated, it is a verifiable fact about a person. This could cover the gamut of information from a person's education level to his or her particular field of study, or from the number of years at his or her former place of employment to the number of different jobs held in the past five years.

In contrast, most psychological/personality questions attempt not to discern facts about a person's past but about how the person might react to situations in the future.

A criterion validity methodology can be constructed using any source of data whether it be psychological, personality, physical, or biographical. However, for the purposes of this book, any reference to a criterion validity study assumes that the study is based on biographical data.

The BCVS is solidly anchored in specific concrete identifiable biographical facts (as opposed to psychological and personality measures) about a person rather than other methods based on vague conjecture or assumptions. Examples of verifiable biographical facts include such items as level of school completed, grade-point average, the person's participation (or lack thereof) in team sports or other extra-curricular activities, and whether or not the person worked to pay for all or a part of their schooling expenses.

By contrast, psychological/personality questions attempt to

provide a basis for hiring in the answers to such probing questions as "Would you rather be a race car driver or a stockbroker? Would you prefer to visit a museum or Disney World? Would you rather be a rocket scientist or a cowpuncher?"

Think of it: researchers have identified over 2,500 biographical facts which can be compiled on any individual. In effect, biographical facts about a person form a unique fingerprint. No two people are alike and no two people will necessarily react identically to the same work conditions. The trick is to match the biographical fingerprint with the characteristics of a particular job. That's the basic purpose of the BCVS.

Unlike psychological and personality tests which are basically descriptive and seldom predictive (description does not always equate to prediction), the biographical validity criterion study develops a biographical imprint of an applicant which has been proven accurate in predicting future success time and again in extensive research.

In order to be most accurate the BCVS should be developed for a specific company environment and the unique employee success factors that contribute to the long-term success of the company as a whole. Remember, just as no two employee biographical fingerprints are identical, no two companies are the same and thus require separate validity studies.

My experience has been that most people have an intuitive belief in biographical factors. The problem is that they tend to focus on the three most identifiable biographical characteristics, which are a person's age, race, and sex. Therefore, they assume that if you can devise a three-by-three matrix using age, race, and sex on the X and Y axis, you can make a valid employment decision. All you have to do is determine which of the nine cells an applicant falls into. Obviously, this train of thought is ridiculous. Remember, there are over 2500 biographical facts about everyone.

A major assumption underlying the BCVS is that biographical facts associated with past behavior often represent the best predictor of future behavior. And, since the BCVS deals with facts as opposed to conjecture, it should help eliminate biases that creep into other selection methods.

In spite of the multitude of biographical facts, there is one classic study which documented the accuracy of prediction for a single biographical item. I was reminded of this study by a recent movie, "Memphis Bell." It is a thoroughly enjoyable film and I recommend it to anybody. It's the story about the final bombing raid of the first B-17 flying fortress to complete twenty-five flights over enemy territory without being shot down. This was no small accomplishment when you consider many of the missions over the European theater suffered fifteen percent casualties or more. The movie especially hit home since my father, Captain Lloyd Mitchell, served as a young navigator of another plane on that very same mission. Fortunately, Captain Mitchell and crew eventually completed their twenty-five missions and returned home unharmed. Otherwise, there would be no Brooks Mitchell to write this book and help you solve your employee selection problems.

The movie reminded me of the landmark pilot selection study, conducted by a team of psychologists after the war and designed to discover what tests were successful in predicting pilot performance during World War II. The government had done a poor job in screening the hundreds of thousands of young men who yearned for the glory of becoming combat pilots and who were subjected to days of physical and psychological testing to help find the best pilot applicants.

The military testing and selection team felt they had an unacceptably poor success rate of pilot selection. After an exhaustive study and much to their surprise, the psychologists discovered that the best predictor of pilot success derived not from the battery of exhaustive psychological and physical tests given the pilot candidates. Instead, the most accurate predictor stemmed from the pilot's answer to a single biographical question on the first application blank completed during the initial visit to the recruiting office.

What was this question that carried such far reaching predictive ability?

Q."When you were a young boy, did you ever build a model airplane that you flew?"

A. Yes——————— *No*———————

A check mark on the affirmative line proved to be the best single predictor of pilot success, and this surprising conclusion created a personnel selection research milestone. This landmark study and the research that followed confirm that biographical facts about people serve as vastly superior predictors of performance, as opposed to their psychological or personality counterparts.

The overall superiority of biographical items as a basis for a predictive model was confirmed by a 1988 study by J.J. Asher which was published in *Personnel Psychology Journal*. Based on a study of many reported selection instruments, he concluded (Figure 7-1) that "in comparison with other factors (intelligence, personality, and aptitude) biographical items had vastly superior predictive ability."

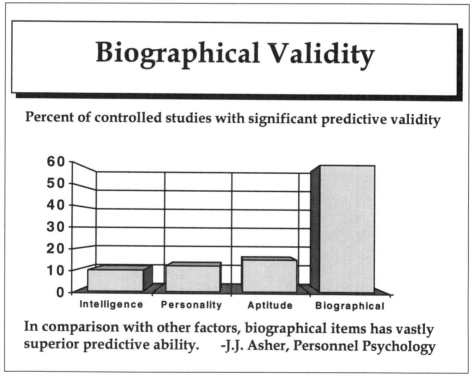

Figure 7-1

Note that in Figure 7-1 biographical studies were almost four times more likely to show a predictive relationship.

One of the main advantages derived from using biographical items is that they are less likely to be faked. One recent review of

150 controlled studies reported that biographical items were seven times more accurate in performance prediction than personality or intelligence items.

Why is this the case? Researchers contend that since biographical items can be readily verified or proven false, employment applicants are less likely to fake these questions than they are to fake personality questions to which they may feel there is a 'best' or 'desired' response.

For example, a job applicant is less likely to give an evasive or false response to "What is the highest level of education you have attained?" The answer can be easily verified by requesting verification from the educational institutions listed. This is in direct contrast to responses to personality questions such as "How many teachers did you dislike?" The applicant can 'adjust' the answer based on how he or she anticipates your desired response.

Obviously, the last type of question is more likely to be faked, thus further distorting the accuracy of most personality tests. Since you can't determine whether or not the respondent's answer has been faked, there is no way to ascertain the validity of the test's predictive ability. Furthermore, the correct response to a biographical inquiry is not obvious if an applicant were prone to try to give an 'expected' answer. To illustrate, using education as a biographical consideration, consider the following question and accompanying answer choices. "What is the highest level of education you have received? a) Did not finish high school, b) GED (Graduate Equivalency Diploma), c) High school graduate, d) Two years or less of college, e) More than two years of college, f) College graduate, and g) Post-graduate education."

Which could be considered the correct response? In reality, who knows? For a specific job, the 'right' answer could be high school graduate while for another position some college education may be desired; and for still another job 'some college' may be detrimental to the applicant's chances of obtaining that opening. An applicant who is trying to second-guess the interviewer or application process could not possibly know what constitutes the correct answer. If he or she assumes that 'some college' experience is desirable, this could, in fact, backfire and remove him or her from the running.

Another plus of using biographical factors to screen applicants arises from their tendency to be less degrading to employee applicants. Instead of starting out the employee/employer relationship with embarrassing or threatening questions, start on a more positive note.

Questions such as "How much have you stolen?" or "Would you take cookies out of your grandmother's cookie jar if you were hungry?" or "How often do you urinate?" accomplish nothing but antagonizing the applicant. (Honest, I have run across this last abomination over the years. That question is between the applicant and his or her doctor and not the company interviewer.)

The degrading nature of test questions was the basis for a successful lawsuit against one of America's best known retailers. This lawsuit, which was settled in August 1993 for $1.3 million dollars, claimed that 704 true/false questions such as "I have never been in trouble because of my sex behavior," "I am strongly attracted to members of my own sex," and "I feel sure there is only one true religion" were a violation of a person's privacy and sex and racial discrimination laws. I agree.

More likely than not, other non-offensive biographical questions would provide the same information as these degrading questions. If you can uncover relationships to areas such as theft or poor performance by biographical items such as education level, number of previous jobs, or absentee history, this will increase the possibility that the employment process can start on a positive and mutually agreeable note. Forget the personal and insulting questions and zero in on predictive biographical items which do not instill animosity at the outset of the employee selection process.

In order for a biographical item to prove most accurate in terms of success prediction, it must be validated for a specific company and for a specific job family within that company. There are no off-the-shelf cures in the employee selection business and no standard biographical items work for everyone.

I am often asked if there are common factors between similar companies in the same industry. The answer is yes, but the companies are different enough to be clearly distinct. I think, when I'm asked this question by executives, it's a thinly-veiled attempt to discover the pill. There is no pill. There are no universals. What works for a similar company will not work for you. It would be the same as saying, "I have heart problems and I want the same heart pills that you gave my friend." That would be foolish and possibly fatal.

In addition, a biographical study within the same company might need to reflect differences in departments and geographical differences, both domestically and in the international arena in which American businesses now compete and draw employees. Different companies possess different corporate cultures, even companies operating in the same industry and serving the same customer base. Success factors and biographical items which accurately predict employee success for Company A would not necessarily work at Company B.

Recent research indicates seven moral regions exist within the United States. Imagine a biographical item related to a New York applicant and transferring it across the board to a California applicant. The terms Valley Girl and Surfer Boy did not spring out of California without good reason. The existence of an array of job family, departmental, corporate, geographical, and moral biographical factors illustrate the complexity of the biographical criterion validity study and why it must be specifically tailored and highly focused.

One retail chain, Younkers, headquartered in Iowa, found that the differences were not geographical but were customer-based. In other words, they found the distinct profile that delineated their large downtown stores or mall stores and their rural stores. There are three clearly different profiles for each of these stores.

The crux of the BCVS lies in the fact that it explains relationships, not causality. To illustrate (although car ownership would not be a question that would be within the parameters of EEOC guidelines today), one employer believed that car ownership related directly to job tenure. More specifically (and this related to the question the company had on its application blank), if an applicant owned a car, the company assumed that he or she would turn out to be a long-tenured person because the car enabled him or her to get to work consistently.

When the company conducted its biographical validity study, it indeed confirmed that car ownership related directly to tenure. Ironically, car ownership correlated with the likelihood of becoming a short-tenured employee! The more employees the company would have hired under their false premise, the more turnover and employee costs would have skyrocketed. And all the while, the human resources people would be telling the boss, "We're really perfecting the hiring process. We've cut the hiring time by twenty-five percent in the past six months." So much for gut feelings and untested assumptions. In six more months, the hiring time would be down to zero because the firm would be forced out of business by high turnover costs and inefficient operations.

The real question remains: How can this situation happen? Believe me, it happens every day across the corporate landscape, costing companies hundreds of millions of dollars annually. The answer lies in the realm of causality. The relationship seemed clear, but why? Well, it should have been obvious. A car provides the road away from an unpleasant job as well as it can transport the employee to the job.

Perhaps those people who did not own cars had to carefully consider the job before they took it, making sure it was the right job for them, since potential transportation difficulties formed an integral part of their decision to accept the job. On top of that, employees without cars tend to experience a harder time finding another job with the right transportation parameters and thus stay at their current positions longer. The key consideration, owning a car, did have a valid relationship to job tenure. The issue revolved around the exact nature of that relationship and the implications for company employee selection assumptions and techniques.

Here's another example of biographical relationships. A corporate study indicated that obese applicants (body weight was a question asked on the application blank) stayed on a sewing machine job longer than their trimmer counterparts. That explained the relationship but where did causality enter the picture? Who really knows?

Anybody with half a brain could come up with any number of reasonable assumptions based on this relationship. Perhaps the obese people felt uncomfortable working in positions with more public contact. As long as they could install zippers in pants efficiently nobody really cared what they looked like. No matter what the real reason, a verifiable biographical relationship existed between obesity and job tenure at the sewing position.

Biographical factors, as mentioned, are relationships; they are not necessarily causality. The car example is a relationship and the transportation issue may be causality. It is interesting to speculate about causality, but one must always do so with a grain of salt. The relationship is real; the causality is speculative.

There are two sources of biographical data, the biographical survey and the job application blank. Data from the biographical survey is usually referred to as a biographical inventory blank (BIB) and data from the job application blank usually results in a weighted application blank (WAB). Both are excellent sources of data for a BCVS.

The BIB usually uses a multiple-choice format and includes a detailed set of biographical questions, often numbering in the hundreds. Both the BIB and the WAB emphasize the determination of factual, verifiable, biographical information. The major advantage of the BIB is that it reveals significantly more biographical data than does the job application blank. The job application blank was never designed with a BCVS in mind, so a researcher is limited to whatever data is consistently available on the application blank.

The BIB, on the other hand, is always designed with a BCVS as its ultimate goal and has the advantage of collecting a large amount of potentially meaningful information. The biggest problem of the BIB is that it is frequently misused (usually inadvertently) in a concurrent validity methodology.

Concurrent validity is a process of dividing existing employees into two groups, good and bad, and administering some type of questionnaire to them. The resulting information is then used as the foundation for a traditional criterion validity study. A concurrent validity is easy for managers to understand and thus has great appeal. Furthermore, the study will usually yield impressive results. Thus, it is a widely marketed and accepted process. Yet, it almost never works in reality.

Why? Because there is a wide gulf between how people will respond to a questionnaire when they have a job and when they are trying to get a job. This is particularly true for psychological and personality tests. Imagine a personality-based question, "How do you like to spend your leisure time?" A job applicant might be much more likely to try to determine the expected response (what are they looking for?), as opposed to a five-year incumbent who might think this is none of their business. The same question, two different perspectives, a statistical difference, no value in predicting job applicants!

The BIB, although far superior to its personality and psychological counterparts, suffers from many of the same concurrent validity problems. For example, it would be awkward to phrase a question such as "Think back to the time when you applied for a job here. At that time, at how many jobs had you been employed in the previous five years, or at that time what was the longest period of unemployment you had experienced?" See the problem with the concurrent validity studies?

The bottom line is that for BCVS information to have maximum value in the real world, it must be gathered from people who are trying to get a job: from applicants who have an intuitive knowledge that their responses will have some bearing on whether they will be offered a job. While this is the most valid way to gather information, it by definition means a waiting period of a minimum of six months to a year in order for the data to mature to a usable point.

Yet, there is a viable source of data for those organizations who don't wait. A readily available source of biographical data appears in almost all job application forms. This data can be recorded and validated using a weighting process which allows the company to score and build a profile containing certain key success factors predictive of future behavior.

The construction of a weighted application blank is straightforward. It is in essence a biographically-anchored criterion validity study. The WAB provides a concrete measuring tool capable of helping to reliably determine the difference between -1 sigma and +1 sigma (Chapter Three) employees, or effective and ineffective employees. Weights are assigned to each biographical item according to the predictive power of the item so that a total score can be computed and compared for each individual applicant.

The first step in a criterion validity (WAB) study is to identify high and low (perhaps high and low performers or long and short tenure) criterion employees (Figure 7-2). Other common variables are people who were caught stealing versus those who were not caught stealing or high customer service and low customer service. After making this determination, the next step compares and scores any measurable biographical differences between the two groups. Usually these differences include identifiable biographical facts from the job application blank or responses to a BIB questionnaire about the employees.

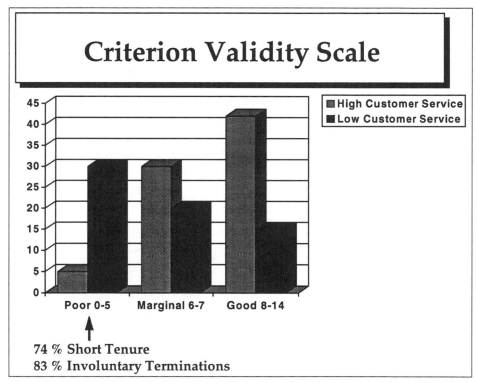

Figure 7-2

The biographical facts from the job application or responses to a BIB questionnaire which significantly discriminate between the high and low criterion groups are statistically combined into a composite scoring model with cut-off scores maximizing the accuracy of the model.

To illustrate, the example in Figure 7-3 is a graphic representation of a WAB scale developed to predict performance which uses three cut-off ranges.

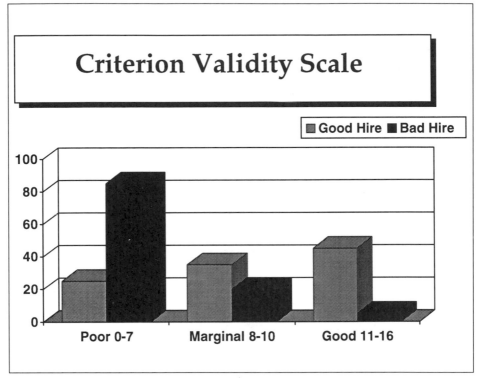

Figure 7-3

Note that in the good range, there are significantly more good performers than poor performers, and that in the poor range, there are more poor performers than good performers. In the marginal range there are approximately equal percentages of both good and bad performers.

The final step in developing the criterion validity scale comes in using the score to predict the high or low criterion status of employees not used in the construction of the survey model. This process results in cross-validation. In other words, if the model predicts the criterion for people not used in the original development, there can be high confidence that the model has utility in a practical application. Cross-validation is also an effective statistical technique for assuring the model is free of disparate impact based on an applicant's race or sex.

In the example in Figure 7-3 the company has a valuable pre-screening tool for job applicants. They also have the wonderful peace of mind that comes from the knowledge that this scale is based on their own organization. It is in effect a statistical mirror of their most recent past. It is not some general range of scores that they have used based on faith and trust in the test vendor. Depending on their applicant flow, they can 'tighten' the cut-off score to increase the probability of success. Or, if faced with few applicants, they will at least know how to maximize their opportunity in the marginal or poor ranges.

Properly developed, a WAB or BIB scale should identify people as scoring in a range. I like ranges as opposed to a specific score because ranges encourage hiring managers to think more broadly about a selection system. A single score on the other hand tends to facilitate a yes or no (black or white) thinking process. In reality, there are usually minimal differences between single scores. So when I am asked, "Is a seven better than a six?" I always respond, "I am not sure, but I know a person in the good range is far more likely to be a high performer than a person in the poor range." Get my point?

Depending on the applicant flow, the best use of the criterion biographical scale is to use it to efficiently 'screen in' a pool of the best applicants. Then each of these applicants should be subjected to a structured interview (Figure 7-4), reference checking, and other company-specific job requirements.

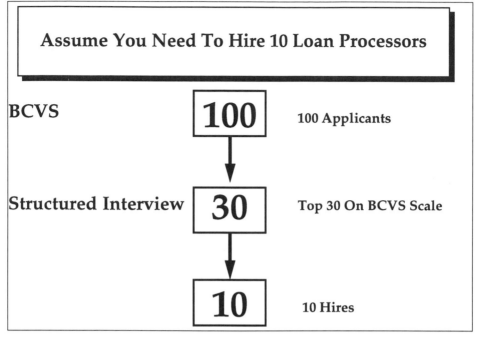

Assume You Need To Hire 10 Loan Processors

BCVS | 100 | 100 Applicants

Structured Interview | 30 | Top 30 On BCVS Scale

10 | 10 Hires

Figure 7-4

As mentioned in Chapter Six, research suggests the ideal ratio of qualified applicants to hire should be three to one. If a company needs to hire ten employees, it could use the WAB scale to identify the top thirty applicants and use other procedures to make the employment decision for the final ten. If you develop a company-specific WAB to identify three applicants for each front-line job opening, and if you use structured interviewing to make your final hiring decision, I can guarantee significant improvements in your hiring results. Furthermore, I can guarantee that nothing, I repeat nothing, can improve your front-line selection results more than this approach!

For most cases, three ranges should suffice: Poor, Marginal, and Good. In a perfect situation, one-third of all applicants would fall into each of these three categories. The Marriott Hotel Division uses the terms red, yellow, and green light to describe these ranges to their managers. I use a fishing analogy to illustrate this concept. Suppose you want to go fishing and you have a choice of Stink Lake, Mud Lake, or Crystal Lake. Notice in figure 7-5 that there are fish and crabs in all three lakes.

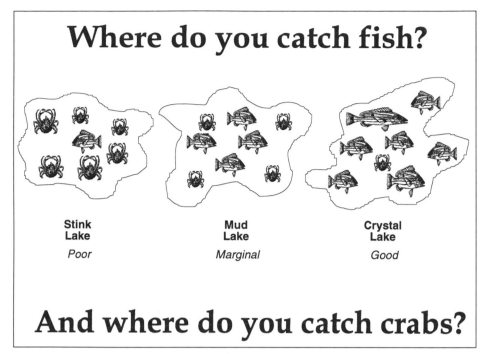

Figure 7-5

However, in Crystal Lake there are significantly more fish than crabs, in Stink Lake there are more crabs than fish, and in Mud Lake there are approximately equal numbers. The question is "Where do you catch fish and where do you catch crabs?" Obviously, if you want to maximize your chance of catching fish, you go fishing in Crystal Lake. However, there's always the possibility that you will catch a crab there. And, suppose, out of desperation, you went fishing in Stink Lake and caught a fish. Does this mean that Stink Lake is a great place to fish? The answer is no.

This is the way a properly developed selection procedure should work It is not perfect; it should simply express the probabilities of hiring a good person in a particular range. The goal of the BCVS based on a WAB or BIB, then, is to help companies identify on a perpetual basis where Crystal Lake is for their jobs.

The WAB process is not new. It has been around since the 1920s when the life insurance industry first used this technique as a way to select agents. The WAB has been the source of numerous research studies and remains the single most documented approach to the improvement of a company's employee selection approach.

Richard Barrett in a 1963 *Harvard Business Review* article stated that "A dismal history has been recorded by personality tests. There have been a few scarce successes with some modern technique; but, on the whole, the typical personality questionnaire test or inventory has not proved to be useful." Precious little has changed since then to change this conclusion about the usefulness of personality tests.

On the other hand, Auralee Childs and Richard Klimoski reported in *Journal of Applied Psychology* in 1986 that even the most rigorous studies using biographical data can, in fact, predict career success. Further adding credence to that claim, Wayne Cascio added, "Compelling evidence exists that when appropriate procedures are followed, the accuracy of biographical data as a predictor of future work behavior is superior to any known alternative."

A number of important research studies reflect that, with proper development and maintenance, the validity of a biographical history item can be maintained despite major changes in the labor and economic markets as well as changes in the internal makeup and environment of the organization. The key issue lies in properly constructing the criteria and biographical information gathering system in the first place and then maintaining it to adjust for changing conditions. As will be discussed in Chapter Eight computers can greatly facilitate this gathering and maintenance process.

George W. England, in his *Development and Use of Weighted Application Blanks* (1971 Revised Edition, University of Minnesota), describes the rationale behind the development of the WAB. According to England the following applies:

1. Personal history information such as age, years of education, and previous job positions represent important parts of an applicant's total background and should prove useful in the selection process. Past behavior represents the best predictor of future behavior.

2. Certain aspects of an applicant's total background tend to correlate to whether or not he or she will be successful in a specific job position. Numerous studies have substantiated the premise that information obtained from employment application blanks can accurately predict successful employees for certain types of positions. Biographical factors such as

previous occupations and level of education correlate with indicators of desirable employee behavior such as previous occupations and level of education correlate with indicators of desirable employee behavior such as tenure, supervisory ratings, and job performance.

3. The WAB helps identify those items on the application blank which differentiate between desirable and undesirable employees in a given occupation.

4. It is possible to assign numerical weights or scores to each application blank answer so that a combination score of the important aspects of an applicant's total background can be determined.

A major tenet behind the WAB process assumes that a clear difference exists between applicants who meet and those who do not meet a specific criterion. For example, employees who quit their jobs within the first three months of employment exhibit different biographical characteristics than those who establish tenure extending beyond one year.

Proponents of the WAB believe the process can identify and quantify those differences and thus establish the probability that a particular individual will meet a certain criterion. In other words, the WAB offers a statistical picture of a person's past and, more importantly, a window into that person's probable future work behavior and chance for success.

It is important to examine the underlying assumptions and rationale for any important course of action. As England states, the WAB process concludes that a person's past activities, actions, and patterns of behavior serve as a useful predictor of that person's future behavior.

It seems logical to assume that the more a prospective employer learns about an applicant's background, the better that employer can predict the employee's future job behavior. Early roots of the reliance on past behavior for the purpose of predicting behavior can be found in the works of Freud and Adler, who developed the lifestyle concept.

Essentially, a person develops a fairly stable style of life. This style is comprised of a set of values, principles, and behavior patterns that the person uses to interpret and react to life situations. The attempt to define and understand a person's lifestyle lies at the center of the WAB development.

An individual's lifestyle manifests itself in a behavior pattern which leaves distinct observable and quantifiable tracks which can be used to predict future behavior. As Edwin Guthrie states, "The outstanding feature of human behavior is its repetitiveness, and repetitiveness is our chief predictive basis when we attempt to describe the nature of man . . . people can sometimes be trusted to do the expected thing in a large variety of situations."

England stresses that the intelligent development of the WAB continues to rely on the three hallmarks of progress in selection: standardization, quantification, and understanding. Although the WAB is far from perfect, it has brought the selection process out of the category of pure chance.

The gambling or pure chance analogy fits. Most businessmen realize that business entails certain risks and gambles in almost any decision-making process. Risks apply to employee hiring decisions and the WAB represents a method to define the parameters of those risks. With a properly constructed and administered WAB, a manager can state with a degree of accuracy that the probability of a particular applicant's staying on the job for a year is .5 or .3 or whatever the WAB score registers.

As another attractive feature, the WAB also ranks high in consistency. In these days of Uniform Employee Selection Guidelines, the Civil Rights Act, and other nondiscrimination legislation and regulations, it is imperative that companies maintain a policy of fairness and consistency for all job applicants regardless of race, sex, age, religion or national origin.

Finally, the WAB provides an effective tool for prescreening large numbers of applicants for a few job openings. This process allows the company to rationally reduce the number of applicants to a manageable number which can then be called in for further consideration.

One of the primary focuses for WAB methodology has been job tenure. Two reasons account for this. First of all, excessive turnover costs employers untold millions of dollars annually and the troublesome problem persists across many industries. Second, tenure information is easy to define and accumulate. Either the employee quit or stayed on the job and the period of tenure falls easily out of corporate personnel records. Even a one percent reduction in a firm's attrition rate can slash thousands of dollars from the labor and other operating expenses.

The WAB approach takes a proactive stance to reducing employee turnover by addressing the problem before the fact. It assumes that high employee turnover can best be reduced by improving the hiring process. This is in contrast to a predominant view which attempts to reduce turnover by changing many of the organizational variables. Remember, it is easier to change who you hire than it is to change the organization.

Alan Schuh (1967) looked at twenty-one studies using biographical data and found that nineteen of them confirmed strong relationships between biographical items on the application blank and tenure. Another study by J.J. Asher (1972) reviewed eleven different studies (different than those analyzed by Schuh) and determined that biographical data in all of them were found to predict tenure accurately. Still another study positively correlated short tenure with poor customer service. Without a doubt, tenure ranks as a valuable variable at the lower level of the organization and deserves even more in-depth research.

The relationship between tenure and customer service was demonstrated by Foley's Department Stores who have used our computer-assisted employment interview tool for over seven years. In a review of turnover of their sales staff over the most recent three-year period, Foley's experienced a thirty-seven percent decrease in their ninety-day turnover.

To help the firm improve the quality of its sales associates and boost employee retention, we constructed a criterion validity study using the computer interview responses for the company's eighty diamond star employees (the highest level of customer service sales associates) and seventy-nine non-diamond star employees. This helped us determine which of the biographical items in combination could best predict diamond star status.

We then performed chi-square analysis (see Appendix A for a

discussion of chi-square) on each question. From this base, we selected seven questions and combined them into a comprehensive profile with a point range of zero to fourteen. This was then incorporated into our computer-assisted employment interview and scored as follows:

Scale: 0-5   Poor
         6-7   Marginal
         8-14   Good

Next, to test the new scale, we screened and hired 172 sales associates for a new store using the new customer service profile. Since no diamond star ratings yet existed for these new employees, we used tenure as the basis for determining employment success: short tenure (any employment terminated before ninety days expired) represented a hiring failure. Likewise, long tenure (employees still employed at Foley's after ninety days) was deemed a success.

Our review yielded two conclusions: 1) seventy-four percent of all associates who terminated in the first ninety days of employment scored in the poor (Stink Lake) range and 2) eighty-three percent of all involuntary terminations were in the Stink Lake range based on customer service.

Consistent with other research conducted by Aspen Tree Software, Inc., this study clearly demonstrated the phenomenon of behavior clustering, that is, that customer service, tenure, and theft terminations are closely related. In other words, good and bad behaviors tend to be clustered. By analyzing this cluster behavior, you can build your own success profiles and improve your hiring track record in several areas.

The phenomenon of behavior clustering was observed and reported in a study in 1988 by Richard Hollinger at the University of Florida. He states, "Among samples of retail and hospital employees, we were able to demonstrate negative correlation between work place attitudes and theft of money from the company. We established an empirical relationship between job dissatisfaction and a number of counterproductive employee activities such as slow or sloppy workmanship, sick-leave abuse, and tardiness."

While most WAB studies cite employee tenure as their primary focus, it can be argued that employee tenure itself serves as a secondary measurement of factors such as productivity and creativity. In other words, employees who did not perform well or exhibit creativity (if that is part of the job requirement) were the most likely short-tenured employees. It also appears reasonable to assume that people with a background history of absenteeism, illness, and pilfering also fall into the short tenure category more frequently. In one study by Rosenbaum (1976), theft was predicted by a traditional WAB study. Thus, the tenure criterion develops into a de-facto measure for many factors other than length of service.

The implications are enormous in the event that honesty tests will probably go the way of lie detector tests. A company that has effective predictors of tenure would also have a de-facto honesty and performance test. Since many companies don't use accurate performance measures, tenure could very well be an accurate substitute index.

Office employees form the focus of many WAB research studies. A WAB study by Johnson, Newton, and Peek (1979) achieved a high correlation of .62 and confirms the usefulness of the WAB as a tool to reduce clerical turnover. They reported that "this study has supported the usefulness of the WAB technique as a selection device in the public sector."

Johnson, Newton, and Peek found validity correlation coefficients ranging from .318 to .73. Similar results were achieved by Fleishman and Berniger in their classic 1960 study. They found a .42 validity correlation coefficient and stated, "the WAB did possess a high degree of validity for predicting tenure."

Shott, Albright, and Glennon (1963) focused on the automated office in their research. They concluded office turnover could be predicted using a WAB and achieved a validity correlation coefficient of .48. Wernimont (1962) examined biographic-demographic data for 206 government service level office personnel. His study was cross-validated and achieved a .34 validity correlation coefficient.

I could continue with study after study after study. I think you get the main thrust of this exercise. Biographical data gathered and validated by the BCVS technique is an effective predictor for job success. You will not find these results for personality, intelligence, or psychological tests.

A biographical validity study or a criterion validity study based on biographical factors needs to remain fluid. A research study by Darrell Roach (1971) indicated a large detriment in predictive power over time due to changes in personnel, policies, management, and selection. Roach concluded that changes in work force, market conditions, manpower requirements, and specific personnel policies combined to create a loss of predictive power. This study reinforces the idea that selection criteria and biographical factors do not remain static.

Edwin Fleishman's (1960) study reached this same conclusion and reported that biographical items deemed to predict success in one job may not possess the same predictive ability for another similar position or for other positions in the same company. All of this reinforces the premise that biographical (or any other) data must be considered for a specific job and for a specific company. This is seldom the case for most commercially available tests.

Further supporting the necessity for staying abreast of the fluid nature of changing selection criteria and their corresponding accuracy, Alan Schuh (1967) reviewed the results of six studies, finding a consistent decrease in predictability. He even recommended further that separate validity tests be considered for male and female workers.

Another caveat in the use of validity studies is necessary. Bass's (1962) research found that study criteria change over time. We operate within a dynamic world. Not only do our work environments change dramatically over time with the introduction of new technologies and new management philosophies, but people's value systems and motivation also change over time.

Simply stated, selection criteria have been, are, and always will be fluid. This fact seems to have escaped a lot of people. There seems to be an assumption that if we can find the key (the pill), then we will have the answer. Well, if you do get the answer, the answer changes, and it changes frequently. To reflect this, a good predicting model should always be revalidated at a minimum of once a year.

Even the weights of the biographical items change with time. Steven Brown (1978) concluded that while the overall validity of a WAB remained the same, a re-weighting of biographical items could occur. In fact, proper monitoring of changes in the weighting of biographical items promised to enhance the predictive power of the biographical survey. Brown further indicated that consistency of biographical predictive items could be improved if the scoring key remained confidential.

Think of selection criteria as a moving target. You have to adjust your sights over time and changing conditions. As the successful profile moves and changes, it is important to continually re-analyze and revalidate in order to reflect those moves and changes accurately.

As emphasized earlier, past behavior predicts future behavior. That's the reason for the emphasis on ferreting out biographical information which predicts employee success for a particular job position in a specific work setting.

Establishing proper criteria forms a keystone in the employee selection process. Each company's unique corporate culture and specific job requirements forge a set of criteria that cannot be duplicated for another company. That's why off-the-shelf employee selection programs are doomed to fail. You must create company-specific, even department- and job family-specific criteria and associated biographical items in order to improve your odds of hiring the right people the first time.

Nearly fifty years ago, Stuit and Wilson (1946) pointed out that researchers need to continually strive for improved performance measures (criteria) in efforts to improve the predictability of success. Without good criteria which measure an important organizational outcome, you can never develop an effective selection procedure.

Criteria represent optimum results, goals which we strive to achieve as probabilities of success in the employment arena. Just as there is no pill to solve your employee selection problems, there is no common criteria which meet the needs and goals of every company.

There has always been an academic problem with the definition of a hiring criterion. The differences have evolved in two distinct camps, those who advocate a composite criterion (such as ninety-day tenure, job performance, sales, etc.) and those who insist that job performance is a multi-faceted phenomenon and thus the hiring criterion should be based on a multiple (as opposed to a single) criteria.

89

Schmidt and Kaplan (1971) contend that the two groups differ in their underlying approaches to the validation process itself. Composite advocates assume that the validity process stems from practical and economic reasons. On the other hand, the multiple advocates see increased understanding as an important goal of the validation process equal in stature to the practical and economic goals.

Proponents of the single composite argument state that even if single criterion elements are used separately in validation, they need to be combined in order to make proper evaluations and predictions regarding the individual by using a composite score. Multiple criteria advocates argue that the combination of positive, negative, and zero variable measurements results in ambiguous scores which cloud the issue rather than presenting a clear picture of probable success predictors.

Personally, I am a strong advocate of the composite criterion approach to selection. Why? Because regardless of the number of criteria you measure, ultimately you still have to make a single decision: To hire or not to hire. This is a composite decision. You either do or you don't. You can't be a little bit pregnant. You are or you are not.

Furthermore, the concept of behavior clustering tends to mitigate the effects of most multiple criteria. For example, a composite criterion which measures short tenure will probably also measure poor performance, poor customer service, and even propensity to steal. This being the case, the composite measure of tenure is a de-facto multiple measure of several other behaviors. I rest my case.

Typically, the gathering of biographical data takes one of two approaches: the weighted application blank (WAB) as discussed earlier, and the biographical application blank (BIB). The weighted application blank was the source of study for my doctoral dissertation, part of my on-going search for the Holy Grail. I conducted a classic weighted application blank study and combined it with a computer to score the WAB and installed it in a large garment factory in the upper midwest. We developed accurate scoring ranges to predict sewing machine operator tenure. When the system was installed I gave my standard speech, that it was in fact just a system,

90

and no system should allow for the elimination of good judgment. In other words, if someone scores well on the WAB and has two heads, don't hire them.

Well, the plant manager (Pete) apparently didn't want to change his hiring technique. When I said that judgment is important, Pete thought (as I imagine it) "Ahah! I've got it! I'll interview these people via the computer. I'll look at their WAB score and then I'll hire them the way I always have in the past." The way that Pete had always hired in the past was judging by the length of a person's fingers, or the stubby finger rule. Pete had told me at the bar that he had determined through years of garment industry experience that people with stubby fingers could not do very well.

Pete used the system and used good judgment because his boss had paid a handsome sum for it, but still let his judgment override everything. I wasn't aware that Pete was doing this until I came back to do a complete analysis a year and a half later. I was very irritated that Pete had hired people in all five of the WAB ranges. Obviously stubby fingers had an equal distribution in society, for whatever that information is worth. I was very irritated and I explained this to my brother, Dr. David Mitchell. He was the one who enlightened me and said, "Brooksie, in fact, Pete has done you a favor."

"Why?"

"Well, because, by hiring people in all ranges, it should be easy to demonstrate the effectiveness of the WAB. In other words, those people in the lower ranges should not have performed as well as those in the higher ranges or should have higher turnover rates."

This turned out to be exactly the case. I realized then that I had the perfect opportunity to conduct research for my doctoral dissertation. For a while I mused about calling the dissertation "The Distribution of Stubby Fingers and Their Relationship to Sewing Machine Success."

I clearly demonstrated that the criterion validity scores could in fact predict tenure for that specific location. It was almost a perfect dissertation because the only time you can ever prove that a selection system is ultimately working or not is to hire people that you assume will fail and see if they do in fact fail. Pete had conveniently done this for me. All of the employees were hired by the same people, worked at the same place, been trained by the same supervisors, got the same benefits and had the same working conditions. The only external variable was their WAB score. The following is a graph which represents turnover results by WAB score.

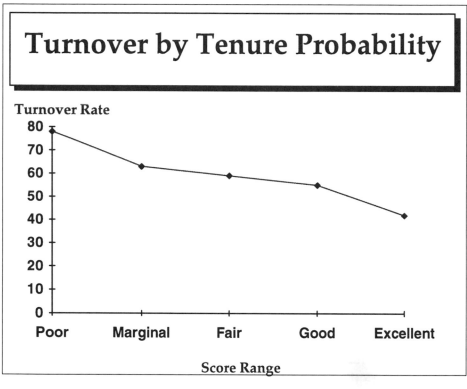

Figure 7-6

Originally, the most popular method for developing a biographical inventory had been through the use of a weighted application blank (WAB). Just what is a WAB? It is a criterion validity method for scoring an application blank by assigning numerical weights (numbers) to job applicant responses on the application form.

Under the WAB approach, a weighted scoring key was developed based on the empirical association of the response options to a certain criterion in order to provide the best prediction of that criterion. To illustrate, a WAB study for an organization might reflect that applicants who are presently employed experience lower turnover rates than applicants who are not currently employed. Therefore, an applicant who is employed would get a 'weight' of two points in contrast to their unemployed counterparts who receive zero points for that question. The WAB study would also indicate the total number of points necessary to maximize the probability of a correct hiring decision given the company's employee success factors and specific criteria.

Criteria commonly used as accurate predictors include turnover, job performance, and theft. In our efforts to help our clients hire the best, Aspen Tree Software has conducted over 150 WAB studies for a wide range of companies and job positions. There is no off-the-shelf WAB that will meet your company's unique requirements and needs. To be most effective, the WAB needs to be developed for a specific company and a specific job category.

Even though a score is compiled based on the weighted criteria, the WAB interview technique does not yield a grade in the traditional sense. Memories of high school, college, and graduate school conjure up nasty images of passing and failing, As and Fs. An applicant completing our interview process does not pass or fail or even receive a grade. No one can tell you that an applicant who receives a score several points higher than another applicant will be a better employee.

Instead, the information provided by the applicant as a result of answering the interview questions is used by the interviewer as a tool in the structured interview process, which we will discuss next. The interviewer is now able to zero in on the relevant areas of concern regarding that specific applicant and job position right from the beginning of the face-to-face interview.

The use of the WAB has been refined over the years to aid prediction success. Owens (1976) advocated a rational analysis approach to the biographical data collected. Under this approach, a conceptual framework or underlying theory guides the instrument construction. In other words, inventory items are selected *a priori* to measure constructs believed to be related to the criterion. Factor analysis is then applied to derive scores that are then related to the criterion of interest. Now, significant relationships can be readily recognized, understood, and interpreted.

Unlike results from personality inventories, data obtained from both WABs and BIBs are unlikely to be falsified. A recent study released by the federal government's Office of Technology Assessment (OTA) on the value and accuracy of paper-and-pencil honesty tests casts considerable doubt that so-called honesty personality tests deliver the results their vendors claim.

In summary, the OTA states, "The existing research is insufficient as a basis for supporting the assertion that [paper-and-pencil honesty tests] can reliably predict dishonest behavior in the work place."

In other words, the results of the OTA study proved inconclusive. The OTA cited the reluctance of test developers to share their data with independent researchers for objective evaluation as a reason for the inconclusive results. Without a doubt, independent corroboration remains a primary prerequisite for good research.

Some recent studies have shown a degree of correlation between integrity tests and stealing, yet many of these tests are based on admissions of theft or lie detector results which in and of themselves are suspect. Therefore, the evidence for the reliability of honesty tests is still inconclusive, at best. There have been some breakthroughs in correlating dishonesty with certain factors, however. For instance, several studies successfully correlated dishonesty with factors such as poor customer service and short tenure. An employee with a tendency to be short tenured also would be more likely to steal in the work place. Therefore, a scale or score developed for a company to predict tenure many times also accurately predicts the possibility of employee theft. This leads to the question that if you can develop a method to predict both tenure and employee theft simultaneously, why engage in the unpleasant aspects of honesty testing?

To be marketed effectively most paper and pencil honesty tests must be generic; in other words, they cannot take into account the environment and circumstances unique to your organization. In addition, most generic honesty tests ask applicants to respond to as many as 200 questions. This is in direct contrast to accepted statistical test development procedures which seldom require this many questions. In fact, maximum prediction accuracy can frequently be achieved with as few as six to twelve items. The only logical reason I can determine for the excess number of questions on honesty tests is that nobody in their right mind would pay what the honesty test vendors are asking if they only included ten or so questions. The number of questions rests more on marketing considerations than on good research practices.

In contrast to generic honesty tests, Richard Rosenbaum (1976) reported on a study of a predictive criterion validity study using job application biographical items for a specific firm, a large retailer, in determining the probability of employee theft. Rosenbaum clearly demonstrated that this methodology predicted a significantly higher percentage of employee theft. In recognition of the correlation between biographical factors and employee theft, the OTA report stated, "There has been a substantial increase in the number of studies which show significant correlation [with integrity] with absence, turnover, grievances, and supervisory ratings."

With that being true, it makes good sense for employers to develop dependable predictors for measuring such performance outcomes. If turnover rates, for example, prove to correlate positively with employee theft, the advantages of developing these predictors would be numerous.

Users of this WAB process compared biographical responses on application blanks of two different applicant groups: those who had been successful and those who were not successful. Then, using a paper-and-pencil template, the evaluators developed a system which called for "adding two points for this, subtracting a point for that, etc."

While numerous research studies confirm the WAB's effectiveness in predicting successful employees, several serious drawbacks detract from its overall applicability. Every employee selection technique comes with some drawbacks and the WAB is no exception.

First of all, selection of specific measurement criteria entails a certain degree of difficulty. England stresses that "careful measurement of the criterion cannot be overemphasized since the value of the entire study is dependent on the adequacy and accuracy of the criterion." Blum and Naylor (1968) take an even more stringent stance: "The criterion is basic to a measurement in Industrial

Psychology, and to overstate its importance would be literally impossible." Thus, a weakness in the use of the WAB approach stems from the difficulty in obtaining clean and precise measurements of almost any criterion. This is a major reason why I like to use tenure as a criterion. As has been demonstrated, it is related to other important criteria and it is easy to define and measure.

A second problem with the WAB methodology arises from the need for many subjects in order to achieve validation and subsequent cross-validation. England stipulates a need for at least seventy-five subjects in both the high and low criterion groups. Without a doubt, finding enough subjects for a given category provides a challenge. Therefore, the WAB often applies to situations where a large historical data base already exists, or where they will be available.

The scarcity of adequate biographic and demographic data, as mentioned earlier, also complicates the construction of a valid criterion model. Few, if any, job application blanks were developed for the purpose of developing a WAB. Therefore, the critical information needed to construct a viable WAB remains lacking in many instances. This particular problem gets compounded with the many changes of application forms over a period of years. Without consistency among various application blanks, many items may have to be discarded in the construction of the WAB, thus compromising the opportunities for cross-validation.

Another problem with the development of the WAB arises with the occurrence of contingency items. For example, responses to a question regarding the number of weeks an applicant has been unemployed will be contingent to a large part upon a previous question regarding present employment status. A careless researcher, not aware of the contingency relationship, could assign weights to both items and thus compromise the usefulness of the WAB. While some contingency items are fairly obvious to researchers, a number of contingency situations remain much more subtle and undetectable by untrained researchers.

In most real world applications, the WAB fails the confidentiality test. Once you construct a paper-and-pencil template and pass it out to your managers, they automatically know what score relates to success. Your managers now engage in subtly and not so subtly coaching applicants on how to respond because they feel the intense pressure to fill the open job positions and get their work force back up to required levels.

For instance, a manager handing an application blank to a prospective employee may say, "Be sure to fill out every item," with full knowledge that failure to completely respond to a certain item results in the application of negative points to the applicant's score. Or the manager might say, "You're going to school, aren't you?" To which the applicant responds, "No." Then the manager says, "Well, wasn't that you I saw in Sunday school last week?" "Oh sure, I guess I am going to school," reasons the applicant.

What, on the surface, seems like an innocent exchange of chit-chat results in skewed and erroneous employee evaluations if 'currently going to school' represented a biographical item which received a weighted score. Based on the fifteen-second conversation, the applicant now receives two points for attending school when in reality he or she should rate a zero score on that particular biographical item.

In the same vein, managers do not understand how the biographical items are derived. In many instances, the biographical items and their weightings can run counter to the manager's own gut feelings and beliefs This results in coaching and can actually be detrimental to the applicant's getting offered a job position. Instead of helping the applicant get over the application blank hurdle, managers end up skewing the results on the negative side. The end result: your company loses the opportunity to hire qualified people with a good chance of success in your organization.

For example, take the following biographical item found on most life insurance industry weighted application blanks.

Q. Have you ever sold life insurance?

   a) Yes b) No

Or

Q. How many years experience have you had selling life insurance?

   a) Less than one

   b) One to three

   c) Three to five

d) Over five

There is no uniform correct answer for all life insurance companies. For one company, previous life insurance sales experience may correlate with short tenure while for another company the desired life insurance sales experience level falls within the three- to five-year experience grouping.

Many managers feel any previous life insurance sales experience ends up being detrimental to salesperson's success in their organization. They prefer to train new salespeople their own way without the complication of previously conceived ideas on how to sell insurance products. Yet a biographical study from application blank data could reveal that for a specific company previous life insurance sales experience of less than three years represents a positive item in the biographical profile of employee applicants.

In one study by Lawrence, Salsburg, Dawson, and Zachary (1982) managers were asked to predict twelve factors used in the hiring decision process that accurately predicted tenure and performance. Only three of the items that the managers picked showed a positive correlation, four possessed no predictive value at all, and five exhibited a negative correlation to tenure and job performance. Chalk up another disaster for gut feeling and intuition.

A true biographical validity study can incorporate several different variables. The human mind can usually incorporate one or two, or three at the most. If a person has three ideas as to what constitutes success, how does he or she evaluate a person strong in two attributes but weak in the third? A properly constructed and implemented validity study using biographical factors can accomplish this task without any trouble.

Another problem with traditional WAB studies stems from the incomplete gathering of application blank data, making it extremely difficult to find items that correlate with success. Application blanks were never designed to gather biographical data, so any information derived from them is incidental. Furthermore, over the years many companies changed their application blanks resulting in researchers being thwarted in gathering historical information on items which might be correlated with success since many of the original application blanks did not request information on certain specific items. In addition, a lack of consistency among companies and the type and depth of applicant information gathered on application forms even further restricts the researcher's ability to find items that correlate with success.

Finally, since the people who interpret the WAB data results in the real world often differ from those who developed the WAB in the first place, the opportunity for misinterpretation exists.

In spite of this fact, job application blanks still provide a very useful source for those companies that wish to develop an immediate criterion validity score. This can be effectively accomplished as long as companies realize that the data is limited and it will take time to gather more complete information. The use of the computer to track and score biographical data delivers some very distinct advantages that help counteract the disadvantages discussed above.

The BCVS, WAB, or BIB can form an integral and useful tool in your company's employee selection process but only with careful development and implementation. The problems discussed above can be overcome by recognizing and understanding the problem areas and by proper planning.

To summarize, a successful BCVS based on a WAB or BIB must be based on the accurate measurement of a standardized criterion. Standardization is seldom achieved by most companies. As reported in *Personnel Psychology*, a 1986 survey of Fortune 1000 companies found that less than fifty percent of surveyed companies provided standardized training for their recruiters.

Instead of focusing on key behavior factors, interviewers concentrated on impressionistic criteria often irrelevant to predicting future success such as the applicant's appearance or his or her degree of enthusiasm (insinuating enthusiasm can be measured in degrees). I think that harkens back to believing in one's gut feeling about a particular job candidate.

Unfortunately, many companies still employ selection techniques which short-circuit or ignore the importance of biographical items. Without objective data to consider, even seasoned interviewers and those trained in traditional interview techniques (Janz, 1982), concentrated mostly on applicant opinions and generalities versus what the applicants had actually done in the past.

Now that we have established the importance and corresponding problems with the development and use of biographical items in the successful employee selection process, we will take a look at some solutions in the following chapter.

I will demonstrate how the WAB and BIB and biographical validity studies can be significantly enhanced by the use of the computer. Aspen Tree Software has developed statistical programs and processes which integrate this valuable technique with the structured interview through the computer. It is as simple as combining chocolate and peanut butter to create a peanut butter cup.

B.J. & Bubba
Cowboy Tips On Employee Selection

Admire a big horse, saddle a small one.

Chapter Eight

THE COMPUTER INTERVIEW

*"If you want a cowboy to give you a straight answer,
look him in the eye and ask him the question."*

Years ago while working at PepsiCo, I wondered, "Why couldn't a computer perform the preliminary job interview?" Upon analysis, I found there were no valid reasons for a computer's inability to accomplish what is required in that initial screening interview. So I set to work developing what is now an expert computer system. It allowed companies to take their own cultures, corporate structure, and specific job requirements and construct an environment where a computer could conduct the preliminary job interview.

At the time, I knew nothing about computers. I think that was probably a blessing, for it allowed me to think in terms of what I knew about structured interviewing. Although I was convinced my ideas were original, this was not totally true. It so happens that Dr. John Greist at the University of Wisconsin had been doing computer interview research with families of people who were admitted to hospitals for heart problems. His methodology turned out to be very similar to the methodology that we developed for job interviews. So, while the idea of computer interviewing did not originate with me, the application to the job interview situation did. It is important to emphasize that the computer cannot be, at this time, nor should it ever be, the sole interviewer. It simply does things that people do not do very well. For example, a computer cannot think, but a computer can be very consistent in gathering information.

How can a computer conduct a job interview? Here's how it works at Aspen Tree Software.

Step one: An applicant fills out a standard application blank. (Some companies now let the applicant enter the application blank information directly into the computer.) The data entry takes about two minutes of a clerk's or interviewer's time.

Step two : The applicant is introduced to the computer with the instructions that he/she will be asked a series of multiple-choice questions and will be required to press the A, B, C, D, E, etc., key and then the enter key to advance to the next question.

Step three: The applicant is left alone to complete the interview. In most cases applicants are not told how long the interview will last. They are only told that the computer will tell them when the interview is complete. In all cases applicants are told they will meet with a live interviewer when the computer portion of the interview is complete.

Step four: The applicant proceeds with the interview. A typical series of questions might be:

John, are you presently employed?
    A.   Yes
    B.   No
    C.   Yes, but I plan to quit
(If B. - No,) John, how long have you been unemployed?
    A.   Less than 4 weeks
    B.   4 to 6 weeks
    C.   6 weeks or longer
(If C. - 6 weeks or longer,) John, how many job interviews have you had in the six weeks or longer that you have been unemployed?
    A.   None

B. One
C. Two
D. Three
E. Four or more
F. I don't remember

(If B. - One,) John, you have had only one job interview during your unemployment. What is the primary reason for this?

A. I took some vacation time.
B. There are no jobs open which require my skills.
C. The state employment agency has not referred me to many job openings.
D. I really don't know why I have not had more job interviews.

John, what is the status of the one job interview you have had?

A. I wasn't offered the job.
B. I was offered the job, but I turned it down.
C. I haven't heard from the company.
D. I was offered the job, but I wanted to see what this job was about.

(If B. - I turned the job offer down,) John, why did you turn the job offer down?

A. It wasn't enough money.
B. I didn't like the hours of work.
C. I didn't like the company.
D. It was a combination of A, B, and C.
E. It was something other than any of the above reasons.

(If A. - Not enough money,) What was the salary for the job you turned down?

A. Less than fifteen thousand dollars per year.
B. Between fifteen and twenty thousand dollars per year.
C. Over twenty thousand dollars per year.

(If C. - Over twenty thousand dollars per year,) John, the maximum salary for the job for which you are applying is eighteen thousand dollars per year. Are you still interested?

A. Yes
B. No
C. Maybe

In the above sequence of questions, the applicant quickly realizes that questions are contingent on previous answers. In other words, the question branching capabilities of the expert software allow the computer to closely approximate the questions a live interviewer should ask. And, if each interview is properly constructed using company experts, it is possible to have the best company interviewer probe every applicant the same way every time. That is maximum reliability and effectiveness.

While the computer does not replace the need for human interaction in the interview process, it eliminates the need for humans to perform those parts of the interview process they don't like to do.

As an added bonus, it ensures that all of the right interview questions get asked of the applicant. Unlike its human counterpart, the computer does not forget to ask a question or fail to follow up with the proper question after a specific answer to a previous question.

Q. What is the biggest barrier to getting honest applicant answers to an interview question?

A.   Getting interviewers to ask the question.

For example, if you asked an applicant why she left a previous job and she said that she was dismissed, what would be the next logical question? Why, of course. The computer will automatically be prompted to ask "Why?", whereas the human interviewer may get sidetracked by a telephone call and forget to come back to that question later in the interview.

That leads us to the computer-assisted employment interview. I was convinced that problems inherent in the traditional paper-and-pencil WAB process and inadvertent application coaching could be eliminated through the use of the computer. For example, I was sure the computer would allow collection of enough data to ensure construction of a statistical profile of the high turnover employee.

It all started back in March 1978 when an applicant for a sewing machine operator job at a large plant was asked to answer some pre-employment questions by entering information directly into an Apple II computer.

The questions were biographical in nature and were an addendum to a weighted application blank process I designed. The intended purpose of the exercise was to reduce employee turnover for this employer. This young female applicant proved to be the first person in the history of the universe to be interviewed for employment using a computer. The rest, as they say, is history.

Over the years, computer-assisted interviewing has garnered a solid foothold in a number of venues. According to a report in American Demographics, computer-assisted interviewing is being used more often by large survey organizations. The reasons are simple, but the advantages are unique. Computer-assisted interviewing allows for self-administered interviewing and the questions and their presentation are standard, making for easy evaluation.

In addition, since the computer questionnaire gathers more applicant information than is required to score the WAB, applicant coaching is virtually eliminated because it would take a German cryptographer to decode the real success algorithms.

We wrote a computer program which asked a series of multiple-choice questions about the applicants. I then conducted an analysis to determine the effect the computerized WAB was having on sewing operator tenure at the company. As expected, we found a direct correlation between high WAB scores and low employee turnover.

Now you may ask, "Won't we find resistance to using an impersonal computer to conduct part of our interviewing process?" On the surface, that appears a reasonable consideration. However, in reality, we find just the opposite reaction. People actually prefer to answer questions using the computer and in today's computer literate world, very few applicants encounter any trouble operating the computer during the interview.

In the early stages of the computer interview, we used to ask people, "Do you like this method of gathering information?" We analyzed results of 10,423 interviews. Of that number, ninety-one percent said they liked the computer interview, three percent said they didn't like it, and the remaining six percent indicated a neutral feeling. It could be argued that people who are applying for jobs would have to say they liked the method; however, this conclusion is 100% consistent with the anecdotal reporting of the interviewers. They all said the computer interview was rated as a highly positive process by the job applicants. This is consistent with Dr. Greist's research.

This represented a real breakthrough in the field of employment selection. Many of us had already recognized the enormous potential of the structured employment interview in helping to hire the right people, but it was cumbersome. Paper-and-pencil questionnaires rarely gathered the right amount of information to construct an accurate success profile. Structured job interviews proved to be very time-consuming, taking as much as one and one-half to two hours to conduct properly. And human interviewers routinely failed to ask the right questions or let personal biases enter the interview process.

The computer allows companies to let the applicant provide data to specific questions and follow-up questions while company personnel go on about their business. Important information does not get left out because the computer does not forget. Equally important, WAB score results remain bias-free because the computer does not possess prejudices or react to an applicant's dress, height, weight, race, interview manner, or other appearance attributes.

The computer also delivers substantial time savings since it can ask more questions in the same amount of time than a human can. The computer does not waste time chatting about the weather or latest sports scores, either.

One study conducted by Dr. Hugh Angell at Duke University indicated that the computer will gather three times as much information as its human counterpart during the same time period. Typically, we have found that the computer interview takes thirty minutes; thus, job interviewers receive ninety minutes worth of information. At the time of the computer printout, the investment in an applicant is generally less than two minutes. I think this is a good trade: ninety minutes worth of information for two minutes worth of time.

The structured computer interview also delivers other benefits. It interprets the applicant's responses and selects a series of open-ended probe questions. These probe questions are then organized into a structured interview format to be used in the person-to-person interview conducted by the line manager.

Armed with this tool, if the manager can read and follow step-by-step directions, he or she (with minimal training) can conduct a complete individualized interview of every applicant. Research has consistently demonstrated that managers who use the computer-generated structured follow-up interview make better hiring decisions. And should this conclusion be a surprise? Remember the research study by Wiesner and Cronshaw (1988) that indicated that significant improvements could be made in the hiring success rate by use of a structured interview.

In fact, based on all of my experience and academic training, I will take the opinion of the line manager who has constructed a thorough structured interview over any test score available. There is no substitute for a structured interview by a line manager. For example, an applicant might answer the question "What type of recommendation do you think you would receive from Acme Bricks, your most recent employer? A) Outstanding, B) Above average, C) Average, D) Below average, and E) I'm not sure." The computer could prompt the line manager to ask the question, "Betty, why don't you think you would receive a better recommendation from Acme Bricks?" This is assuming, of course, that Betty said something less than "Outstanding."

Our experience at Aspen Tree has revealed that line managers quickly memorize the questions. Consequently, they're even able to be more relaxed during the interview and listen more carefully. Listening to the applicant's response as opposed to thinking about the next question is a key factor in conducting effective interviews.

Use of the computer eliminates the subjective decision-making resulting from rambling questions asked during a short in-person interview. The computer-assisted interviewer deals with facts, comparing apples to apples.

Of the millions of applicants who have been interviewed by a computer, I am not aware of one single person who refused to be interviewed this way. The computer removes the possibility of unpleasant or negative feedback to applicant responses.

As already discussed, the computer remains free of bias and prejudice. It has no sex, age, race, or annoying mannerisms to contend with. It puts applicants at ease, allowing them to respond honestly to interview questions. There's no need for second guessing the interviewer or trying to make the proper or right response.

Considering that up to one third of applicants lie about job experience on their job application blanks, according to a study conducted by the Port Authority of New York, the honesty issue looms large in the employment interview process. Since research shows that applicants respond more honestly to computers, that fact alone should grab your attention.

One large national chain of grocery stores asked the question via the computer, "Are you honest?" Remarkably, four people hired (out of 2,000 hires) responded they were not honest. Amazingly, all four people were terminated in the first six months for involuntary reasons. The obvious question is: Why did the store managers hire people who said they were not honest? The real reason is that the store manager probably didn't read the interviews very carefully. I can assure you, after revelation of this fact to the vice president, the store manager will very carefully read all interviews in the future.

Why are applicants more honest with the computer? There are three schools of thought on that issue. One school views the computer as a peerless interviewer, ageless and sexless, and thus less suspect and threatening than a live interviewer. People feel more comfortable responding to something which cannot respond. Therefore, it removes the need for socially desirable responses by the applicants.

The second school of thought subscribes to the big brother effect which provides an atmosphere in which the system already knows everything so the applicant need not try to conceal anything with dishonest answers.

Personally, I like the Brooks Mitchell school of thought. I believe that most people are fundamentally honest folks who would like to give an honest answer to interview questions. The problem of dishonesty arises in face-to-face interviewing situations because the interviewer feels uncomfortable asking sensitive questions and the applicant feels pressure to provide the proper answer. Since the computer does not personally care how the person responds and the applicant cannot read anything into the computer's actions or reactions, he or she responds truthfully to computer questions.

Q: What should you do with job applicants who tell the computer they plan on working for your company less than six months?

A: Believe them and don't hire them.

Now why would an applicant admit that he or she only plans to stay on the job for six months or less? Because the computer asked the question. In my years of experience, I find that it is often more difficult to get company interviewers to ask hard, pertinent questions than it is to get applicants to give honest answers once the question is asked.

I think most applicants (myself included) feel that they are not obliged to volunteer less than flattering information. However, most people, if asked, will answer the question. Many years ago, my wife and I had a live-in babysitter. She applied for, and was offered several jobs as a part-time waitress at various restaurants near our home. Amazingly, not a single restaurant asked her how long she planned to stay. In reality, she really only planned to work until Christmas, and then return to her home. I asked her, "What would you have said if they would have asked how long you planned to work?" She said, "I would have told the truth; I am an honest person."

Christopher L. Martin of the College of Business Administration at Louisiana State University at Shreveport and Dennis H. Nagao of the College of Management at Georgia Institute of Technology (1989) researched the effects of computerized interviewing on job applicant responses. The study entailed a laboratory simulation in which subjects were interviewed for either a low- or high-status position (clerk or management trainee) under one of four interview conditions: computerized, paper-and-pencil, or face-to-face with an interviewer who behaved either warmly or coldly toward the applicant.

The researchers concluded that the applicants in nonsocial (computer or paper-and-pencil) interview environments scored lower on the measure of socially desirable responses (SDR) and reported their grade point averages and scholastic aptitude scores more accurately than those applicants participating in face-to-face interview situations.

Martin and Nagao also found that applicants did not differ significantly in their perceptions of how able they were to express themselves during the interviews, how comfortable they felt with respect to the interview procedure, or how well they thought they had performed during the interview. In other words, the applicants did not feel hampered or handicapped by the nonsocial or impersonal nature of the computer interview. In addition, the degree of hands-on computer experience did not impact the expressed comfort levels with the computer interview process or with the results of the applicants' socially desired responses. Although this study took place in laboratory conditions, the researchers found their findings of lowest SDR in the computer interview setting consistent with reports from the real world employment interview situation.

Computerized interviews offer other major benefits over traditional interviewing procedures. As applicant responses are received and analyzed by the computer, immediate follow-up questions get asked to further define a particular response. In this way, the interview gets tailored to the individual.

Time and accuracy also come into play since the computer is pre-programmed to score the applicant's answers. As soon as the applicant finishes responding to the interview questions, the computer instantly delivers an accurate score (assuming a criterion study has been conducted of the responses) ready for review by the interviewer. In addition, we have developed software that enables the computer to prepare a list of questions for use by the interviewer in the face-to-face interview session.

Using this process, the computer chooses each question from a bank of questions based on how the applicant responded previously. The computer can ask three times more questions than can a human interviewer in the same amount of time. Plus the computer checks for contradictions or items that will need to be followed up either with additional questions or as questions prepared for the later face-to-face interview. In that way, all of the bases get covered. There are no gaps in the interview information required to make an accurate and successful evaluation of the applicant.

In other words, if properly constructed by experts, the computer-assisted interview should allow for the best company expert to interview every single applicant the same way every single time. What a tremendous advantage this is. This would be particularly true for a company with many different geographic locations. They would now have total control over the interview process and consequently would be able to improve their hiring decisions.

Computers are making inroads into a number of areas which were previously the realm of human interviewers. Market researchers use computers to assess product demand, product acceptance, and name acceptance. Political pollsters use computers to judge the popularity of political candidates or sensitive political issues.

Among major organizations won over to computer-assisted interviewing are the United States Navy (personnel tracking), the health care industry (to record medical information while a patient is en route to a hospital in an ambulance), the United States Census Bureau (monthly telephone Current Population Surveys), and The National Center for Health Statistics (data collection for its Health Interview Survey). In the medical field, facilities use computers to perform initial patient interviewing, researchers use computers to collect drug use or abuse information from students, and medical personnel use computers to help treat mental disorders.

Today, computer-assisted interviewing is well respected as a valid method of helping predict employee success and hiring the right people for the job. Looking back, it traveled an evolutionary process of thoughts, experience (augmented by education), observation, good common sense, and plain old hard work. There was no pill or quick-fix solution to developing the computer-assisted interview either.

With the proliferation of small and inexpensive personal computers, any company can avail themselves of twenty-first century interviewing techniques to improve their ability to hire and keep the right people.

The computer will never replace the human element in applicant interviewing, but it does efficiently handle the tasks people do not like to do. Unlike humans, computers will never forget to ask a question and computers can collect three times as much information from an applicant as a human can during the same amount of time. Therefore, it is no feat for a computer to organize and ask 125 questions or more while the human would more than likely be overwhelmed.

It also stands to reason that a computer does not get bored interviewing applicants or have outside pressures that get in the way of conducting a good interview. As a result, the computer performs a more consistent job of interviewing.

This meshing of synergistic human and computer abilities produces a highly structured and predictive job interview tailored to meet the specific company's employee needs based on its unique critical success factors.

Dr. John Greist of the University of Wisconsin and his colleagues have been developing computer programs to diagnose a wide variety of major medical disorders. Like employment interviewers, therapists often have trouble overcoming prejudice from a particular school of thought. The use of computers helps eliminate preconceived notions.

One of the best examples of how well a computer can evaluate a person stems from a University of Wisconsin study of potential suicide victims at the university. Psychiatrists and other health professionals were pitted against the computer in attempting to predict which patients in a study group of sixty-three people would attempt suicide. The therapists failed to identify any of the three who would attempt suicide within forty-eight hours, while the computer correctly predicted all three based on responses to multiple-choice questions answered by patients on its terminal. In a three-month study, the ninety-one percent of the subjects who actually attempted suicide had been given a better than even chance of doing so by the computer. In comparison, medical professionals only scored a sixteen percent prediction success ratio.

Returning to the employment selection problem, the use of the computer to ask applicants pre-interview questions can pay off big in terms of enhanced company productivity, lower turnover, and reduced hiring needs. Since the computer can keep track of thousands of applicant responses, it can form a comprehensive database for companies to form a successful employee profile. This database is a tremendous advantage for companies. In fact, one president of a large insurance company said the database on their 20,000 applicants and hires for their company life agents was one of the most valuable properties owned by the company. The database will age over time and can be used for many many purposes, for example, profiles of people who are promoted, profiles of people who became top managers, etc. With today's statistical programs, the database can be easily manipulated by managers without the help of Ph.D. statisticians.

Using computers helps weed out unacceptable candidates (by indicating the location of Stink Lake), saving the company valuable time and resources. It also permits the interviewer to focus on critical success factors in the face-to-face interview.

Computer-assisted job interviewing is rooted in the belief that there is no substitute for a well-structured job interview. As discussed in Chapter Six, The Structured Employment Interview, ample research proves the value of the structured job interview in helping to predict successful employees.

The structured computerized interview works to correct the shortcomings of traditional interviewing techniques:

- forgetting to ask important questions
- letting personal biases cloud the interview decision
- being reluctant to ask sensitive questions
- failing to follow up responses with pertinent questions
- taking too much time to accumulate applicant information

Since the computer generates a list of interview questions, the interviewer is free to concentrate on listening or taking notes, something difficult to accomplish during an unstructured interview. In fact, a line manager, armed with the computer-generated list of open-ended probe questions can do an outstanding job of interviewing the applicant with minimal training. All he or she has to do is simply read the questions with something more than a monotone voice. Contrast this advantage to a previous one- to two-day interview training program that is usually forgotten within a week or two.

By phrasing all questions the same for each applicant, the computer prevents the possibility that the interviewer is discriminating against a particular applicant based on first impressions or personal biases.

Finally, structured interviewing provides a consistent database of information on all applicants so comparisons can be made on an apples-to-apples basis.

The computer organizes the applicant's responses in a fashion that allows you to use them effectively in the employee selection process. It can indicate which responses need to be looked at in more detail during the person-to-person interview. In fact, the computer will even generate appropriate follow-up questions based on the applicant's answers.

For example, if the applicant indicated that he or she is currently attending school, the computer will compile an open-ended question to ask, "How will your working at our company affect your plans to further your education?"

Each follow-up question can be tailored to meet the specific requirements and success factors unique to your organization. The computer could even include a clue or note to the interviewer. For example, "NOTE: Listen to this response to determine if the applicant is likely to quit this job and return to school full time."

Using questions and categories compiled by the computer, the interviewer can focus on areas directly correlated with key success factors in the organization. In addition, the computer saves hours of interviewer time by quickly and easily summarizing basic applicant information such as length of previous employment, education level, etc. Hours of data in minutes of processing time — not a bad tradeoff.

Your computer can also track applicant average response time, indicating whether he or she had to think longer to answer a specific question. Research has shown that it takes most people more time to lie than to tell the truth.

The computer can also detect inconsistent information in responses given to various questions throughout the initial computer interview. Again, the computer will generate the necessary follow-up questions to make sure the discrepancies get resolved to the interviewer's satisfaction.

Computer interviewing can also flag over-responders for more in-depth questioning during the follow-up person-to-person interview. Employee selection research indicates that the person who most often tells you what you want to hear is often the applicant who is not telling the truth.

Over-responding seems to be a manifestation of the old axiom: If something seems too good to be true, it probably is. As mentioned previously, the computer interview flags problems or concerns for applicants. However, practitioners report that someone who does not manifest any problems in the computer interview is probably just as bad as someone who manifests many. This is probably an example of over-responding.

Over the past two years, I have conducted over 200 criterion validity studies which consistently point out that over-responders make bad hires.

To illustrate, assume your interview questionnaire contained the following question and potential responses:

John, how many days did you miss from work last year due to illness?

A. None, I had a perfect attendance record
B. 1-3
C. 4-5
D. Over 5

Most of us would like an applicant to assure us that the only time he or she has ever missed work was when his or her mother died, and even then only for the two hours necessary to attend the funeral. In other words, response A) apparently ranks as the best answer. However, almost every criterion validity study I have ever conducted in decades of experience reflects that applicants who choose response B) have proven to make better hires.

It's easy for me to speculate that applicants who over-respond to the computer interview will probably over-respond during the human interview as well. They will probably look a little neater, talk a little better, and have all the right answers. I am convinced that they bank heavily on the power of first impressions. Unfortunately, many interviewers appear overly attracted to the applicant who seems just perfect for the job.

Equally unfortunate, when hiring decisions stem from appearance and first impressions, the results are predictable and the interview and hiring cycle soon begins anew.

Using a computer in your employee selection process can also work to improve your applicant-to-hire ratio. Recently, I compared some side-by-side (with and without computers) studies of interviewers for two Fortune 500 companies. We discovered that the same interviewers who used computers to conduct structured interviewing one day and used their conventional unstructured interview techniques the next day compiled radically different applicant-to-hire ratios under the two interviewing methods.

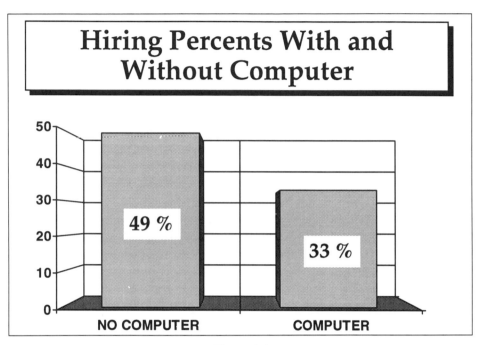

Figure 8-1

When these interviewers did not use the computer, their applicant-to-hire ratio stood at fifty percent. In other words, they hired one out of every two people interviewed. Using the computer interview tool, the applicant-to-hire ratio improved to thirty-three percent. In other words, supplied with more objective data, the interviewers became more selective.

I found this exciting because employee selection research suggests that this three-to-one ratio is optimum. To further test this benefit of using a computer in interviewing, I reviewed data to verify the applicant-to-hire ratios of some other big-time users of our computer employee selection programs and confirmed the same thirty-three percent hiring percentage. Same interviewers, same location, and same success criteria but vastly superior results due to use of the computer in the employee selection process.

That's the magic of the computer-aided interview process. It helps you skim off the three best possible applicants and then lets you pick the best of the three. Creme de la creme.

A ninety-day turnover has been the focus of many companies who use the computer interview. This period forms a crucial component in your strategy to keep your firm's turnover and hiring costs down, for it has been proven that after that time, turnover drops off substantially. Therefore, it stands to reason that if you can segregate the factors that point to applicants who are most likely to leave your employ within that ninety day period, you can improve your hiring retention ratio and slash employee hiring and training costs. You can see from the following graph how turnover in the first ninety days can eat your lunch.

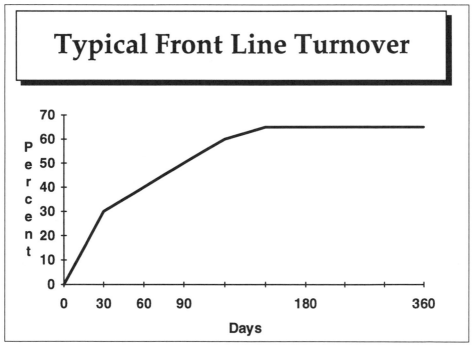

Figure 8-2

That's where the structured interview process and computer-assisted interview come into play. Using a criterion validity study, we can construct a success profile for your firm that lets you segregate applicants into good and bad employee prospects. For each company, the success criteria differ. The criterion validity study can help you narrow down the best applicants for your company, for a specific job family, and even for a specific geographical area. My studies have proven that success criteria for a company's plant in New York more than likely do not work for that same company's plant located in California.

Bad prospects could mean the applicants don't meet certain performance criteria or that they have a high chance of quitting within the first ninety days of employment. On the other hand, good prospects could have just the opposite definition or some other combination of success factors.

I think a few comments concerning turnover are appropriate here. Turnover is particularly expensive at the front-line level of employment. As mentioned previously, some studies indicate there's a close relationship between high turnover, high theft, high absenteeism, and low customer service. It seems appropriate to measure turnover because it is easy to grasp. However, it has been my experience that most companies measure turnover poorly. When I ask them what the turnover rate is, they say it is twenty-five percent. I say, "Where does twenty-five percent come from?" They say, "We took the number of terminations last year and divided them by the average number of people on our staff." A much more sensitive way to measure turnover is by anniversary dates, for example, the percentage of people who completed thirty, sixty, and ninety days. This is more accurate and it holds line managers accountable for the process. Furthermore, as seen in a previous graph, if you can reduce turnover in the first sixty to ninety days, you can reduce the long-range implications of turnover. So, for those organizations who do wish to improve turnover, one of the first things to do is to closely examine the way turnover is measured.

Once you have constructed your success criteria, it's easy to use the computer to conduct the initial employment interview and compare applicant responses with your success profile. Another major benefit of employing your computer power to construct and maintain your success criteria stems from its ability to allow you to fine tune your selection criteria as you move forward.

You compete in an ever-changing business environment. Today's sophisticated statistical computer programs let you factor in changing economic conditions, shifting demographic patterns, and evolving employee/applicant work attitudes and perceptions.

Let's return a minute to the problem of high turnover rates. Faulty interviewing and hiring practices cost businesses millions of dollars every year. Even more frightening, the process repeats itself endlessly unless some corrective action is taken to change the basic premises underlying the hiring process itself.

American General Life & Accident Insurance Company (AGLA) first tested the Aspen Tree Software employment selection program in 1990. According to John Coleman, Vice President of Marketing Administration, "Two things were very apparent to us. We had entirely too much paperwork involved in putting a new agent on the payroll and Aspen Tree's program was the pivotal point around which our employment process revolved. A consolidation program now enables us to transfer data from the computer-assisted employment interview to a database which serves as the driver for other company employment-related systems. In addition to using this employment technique to improve the quality of our new agents, we have a system which decreases a significant amount of paperwork. It's nice to have your cake and eat it, too."

In 1991, AGLA expanded the use of the Aspen Tree employment selection program segment-wide, resulting in an eight percent improvement in agent turnover. Today, AGLA's turnover rate ranks twenty percent better than the industry average. Equally important, the insurance firm's field managers (line managers ultimately responsible for the success of their agents) reported that the interview guide significantly improved their ability to interview and hire successful agents.

The improved turnover experience of our clients and ample turnover research speak for themselves. But the success story does not end there. There's a myriad of benefits you can derive from employing the computer-assisted employee selection process.

In late 1990, we completed the effects of our computer-assisted interview on four outcomes for a telephone operator position: employee turnover rates, employee absentee rates, quality assurance scores, and keyboard test scores. Our study tracked these four performance measures for 551 applicants for telephone operator positions at a major national telecommunications company during a six-month period. Job interviewers hired one-third of the applicants after consideration of the results of the computer-assisted interview. The other applicants were hired using traditional interview techniques.

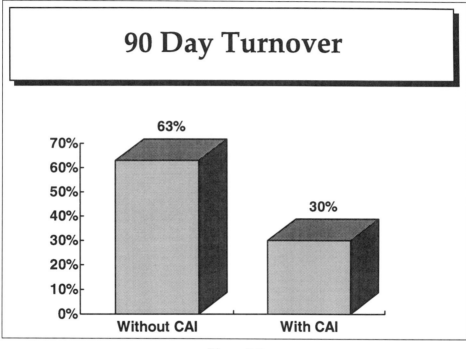

Figure 8-3

Once again, the study showed that applicants hired with the benefit of the computer-assisted interview experienced a thirty-three percent decrease in turnover. In addition to the turnover reduction, employees hired via the computer-assisted interview program demonstrated a one percent improvement in quality assurance scores, tested .69 percent higher on the keyboard test, and decreased their monthly absentee rate from 2.833 days per month to .786 days per month. Once again, the clustering of good behaviors can be predicted and used to improve performance across a wide range of measures.

These benefits are not limited to service firms. Our industrial clients have experienced similar results in operations ranging from

tobacco processing and cigarette production to garment manufacturing, to health care, to fast food and more.

The chart below describes the hiring results of a large retail
organization who tested the computer interview. They installed the
computer interview at four stores and used it to interview all job
applicants for a period of three months. However, the personnel
interviewers were not allowed to see the results and hired applicants as they always had.

Applicants hired who admitted to the computer:	Number hired
They were a convicted felon	7
They planned to stay less than a year	7
Everyone steals from their employer	9
Everyone will probably steal from their employer	12
Seniority should be the primary basis for promotions	8

Figure 8-4

As you can see, they hired numerous applicants who were
probably less than suitable for the job. Why? Because they over-
relied on the unstructured interview and first impressions. Also, a
follow-up investigation revealed they spent only seven minutes
with each applicant. Under those circumstances, how could they
have possibly uncovered the depth of information provided by the
computer which would have given them ninety minutes worth of
human information?

Perhaps the best testimonial to the effectiveness of the computer-assisted employment process comes from our client, Marriott
International. After extensive review, Marriott's Hotel Division

human resources team recommended that the Aspen Tree Software computer-assisted employment interview program be implemented in all of its hotels and reservations centers.

"We had other interviewing systems that were being used at various hotels throughout the company. Therefore, I organized a task force to determine which of these, if any, were useful in improving our ability to select the right candidates," said Richard Bell-Irving, Vice President of Human Resources.

Marriott tested the program in a nine-month in-depth study. According to Bell-Irving, the results showed a dramatic decrease in associate turnover. They also confirmed the close relationship between the profile of a short-tenured person and the characteristics of an employee with poor customer satisfaction skills.

"There were several other valuable conclusions from our study, but I don't want to tip off our competitors," said Bell-Irving.

The value of the Aspen Tree Software computer-assisted employment interview program's ability to generate a structured interview guide was illustrated during an electrical outage in the Human Resources Department at the New Orleans Canal Street Marriott Hotel. The power would not be restored for twenty-four hours, so to keep the interview process on schedule, the Human Resources Department continued to send job applicants to line managers, but without the computer-generated employment interview guide and questions. The line managers responded with a call to the Human Resources Manager saying that they would rather wait a day or two than interview an applicant without the guide.

In summary, the evidence is overwhelming that the computer interview can be of great assistance to humans in conducting the employment interview. However, it is important to stress that the computer can never replace a person. A computer simply can do some things that people don't do very well, and people can do many things that computers can't do very well. We've discussed many of the advantages that are available via the computer; however, a computer will never be able to use empathy, sympathy, reasoning, etc. Perhaps in the future, it will be possible. I don't think it will be possible in my lifetime. The computer is not the pill that we have been looking for, it is simply a tool. Properly constructed and administered, computer-assisted interviews can, however, make significant improvements in the overall employment process.

B.J. & Bubba
Cowboy Tips on Employee Selection

*A cowboy who ain't got ideas of his own
should be mighty careful
who he borrows 'em from.*

CHAPTER NINE

PEANUT BUTTER AND CHOCOLATE

"Don't build the gate 'til you've built the corral."

Now it's time to put it all together, uniting the structured job interview with the biographical study to arrive at a comprehensive and effective employee selection process. You combine two great things and the end result is something much better. Synergy!

Peanut butter and chocolate equals a Reese's™ Peanut Butter Cup. The analogy, of course, is that when you combine peanut butter (the biographical study) with chocolate (the structured job interview), you create a powerful employee selection tool. The end result is something much better and much more effective than merely the sum of each of its parts (Figure 9-1). You develop a synergy that promises to revolutionize your hiring potential.

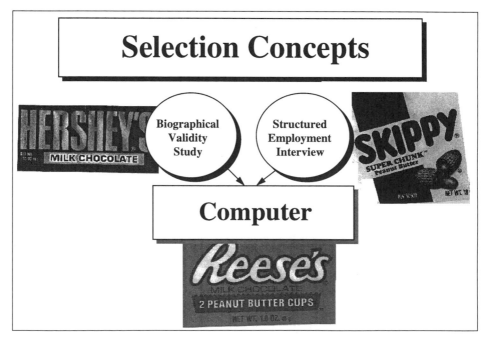

Figure 9-1

Even more impressive, we combine the capabilities of the computer to further enhance employee selection possibilities. In effect, we create a whole new medium for ongoing employee selection research and practical applications.

As illustrated earlier, the use of the computer in the employee selection process for front-line employees accomplishes several important goals. First of all, it collects consistent information on every single applicant, thus helping to eliminate hiring bias. Consistency and reliability, of course, are the first steps towards improving any system. Without fail, every question will be asked of every interviewee. This is a particularly comforting advantage for organizations with numerous geographic hiring centers.

Having different interviewers collect information has always caused problems in research reliability. How can you improve something if you have not standardized it? The computer ensures consistency of data gathering as it is the same for everyone. It does not harbor prejudices or forget to ask questions. The computer gathers information on a discreet basis, branching off to related questions as desired. It then prints out applicable follow-up questions for the live interviewer to ask in the face-to-face interview.

Second, the computer performs many tasks that humans do not do well or do not want to perform. It removes the boredom and routine aspects of interviewing.

And, as it relates to the criterion validity study, the computer interview provides several significant benefits which overcome many of the traditional job application/WAB methodology problems:

1) Responses are much more accurate when gathered by computer as compared with traditional pencil-and-paper techniques.
2) Extensive research has shown that job applicants respond more honestly to computers than they do in traditional interview situations.
3) You achieve a one hundred percent completion rate. Often, applicants answering pencil-and-paper questionnaires fail to complete all questions leaving the interviewer with incomplete applicant data. The computer demands answers to every question.

4) You obtain one hundred percent consistent information, creating applicant data files with maximum statistical reliability as a base for predicting those potential employees with the best odds for achieving success in your organization.

5) The computer format with its ability to prevent erroneous data entry permits you to move directly from interview data to statistical analysis.

6) Finally, and most importantly, the computer allows you to gather this critical information efficiently at the time the applicants are interviewing. This is extremely important because there is a basic difference between job applicants and existing employees. Unfortunately, many managers believe you can interview existing employees and divide them into two groups (good and bad employees) and then draw valid hiring conclusions. This process, called concurrent validity, is very tempting for management to believe; however, it is a very weak foundation upon which to build your hiring program. To be sure, you will arrive at some statistical conclusions based on this methodology, but it will be of little practical value because there's a vast psychological difference in people trying to obtain a job and in those who already have a job. The computer gets the data from people at the time they are interviewing for a job, and that's an important distinction.

Even with all of these impressive benefits, the computer can never replace the live interview process where open-ended questions can delve further into areas of the applicant's background, experience, etc. To be effective, the computer must be used as a tool, not a pill. There are many things computers do better than people, but there are many more things people do better than computers.

We know from research that the computer interview, if properly conducted, should have an applicant on the computer in less than two minutes, and the average applicant time to finish a computer interview falls in the thirty-minute range. Within that thirty-minute time span, the computer will garner an hour and a half of information. In comparison, the human interviewer takes, on average, three times as much time to get the same information that the computer gathers in a half hour. And when interviewers receive the information, they can review the information the way they want to see it, not the way the applicant wants to present it. Based on time considerations alone, the computer interview process makes good common sense. When you fold in all the other advantages discussed above, it should be a 'no brainer.'

In addition, modern statistical programs in tandem with the computer allow for a manageable manipulation and analysis of the data. Recall the studies of Roach and Brown in Chapter Seven, which reported the fluid characteristic of both the predictive items and the weighting of those items. Employee selection criteria has never been and never will be static. Employee selection criteria is a moving target. The computer's ability to perpetually gather and re-validate information in a consistent manner allows a company to stay close to the bulls-eye.

This represents a significant improvement over most current test validation methods which survey (sometimes as long as every ten years) to gather information and then try to make rational conclusions based on that data. Even if a conclusion is valid, it is already aged and been compromised at the time of implementation and will continue to deteriorate over time. And, to complicate matters even more, most tests are validated on industry norms as opposed to the norms of a specific company and job family. I think most test developers know better, but it is easier to sell a test to a company for ten to one hundred dollars than it is to sell a company- and job-specific validation study.

Data gathering capabilities of the computer at the time of the job application greatly improve the data gathering process and subsequent criterion validity analysis. The use of the computer during the information gathering process also aids the accomplishment of other human resources tasks such as accumulating equal employment information required by the Equal Employment Opportunity Council (EEOC). Most of the users of the Aspen Tree Software computer-assisted employment interview simply have applicants enter their race and gender. For example, a typical question would be:

Acme Bricks is required by law to keep certain information concerning your race and gender. This information will not be used in

127

any way other than to prepare these required government reports. You do not have to answer this question if you do not want to.

(Applicant's first name), what is your gender?
A. Female
B. Male
C. I do not wish to respond to this question.

This information makes it possible to prepare instant and accurate EEOC reports. Even more important, this information can be used to insure there is no disparate impact in the computer interview and subsequent validation studies. And, of course, the computer interview code is written to keep this information off the interview report. This helps to insure that interviewers will be able to review and interpret the information without prior knowledge of the applicant's sex and race.

This helps to keep bias from entering the employment picture. The computer does not factor in subjective personal appearance impressions. Research has clearly shown that use of the computer in the interview process helps eliminate biases and helps to keep your employment interviewing objective and out of trouble with the EEOC. Recall the study represented in Figure 5-1 which documented the removal of race bias when interviewers made hiring decisions based on computer-assisted structured interviews as opposed to traditional non-structured methods. Why? Because they evaluated the applicants based on consistent and objective information. The same interviewers, not using computers, hired significantly fewer minority employees than white employees.

Direct hookup into mainframe computer programs delivers even more in-depth reporting and easier use of employment data for various corporate purposes. Virtually at the touch of a finger and within minutes, information on hire dates, termination dates, term codes, and performance data can be constructed in various report formats for a myriad of uses. American General Life & Accident Insurance Company (AGLA) combined the computer interview with several other employment procedures and eliminated over fifteen documents required to put an agent on the payroll.

Continual compilation and expansion of employment data

builds a huge database which becomes increasingly valuable to companies seeking to perfect their employee selection process. But unless you collect this database, your efforts to determine which applicants possess the best chances for success in your company, which employees were terminated for theft, which employees achieved production goals, and which employees proved to be short-term versus long-term will be minimized.

AGLA has been using the computer employment interview since 1989. As reported in their 1991 annual report, their annual agent turnover has decreased by eight percent (their 180-day retention rate has improved even more), and their company rate is now twenty percent lower than industry standards.

Prior to implementing the computer interview as the primary pre-screening technique, AGLA was using an industry-wide life agent test known as the LIMRA Career Profile. A quick chi-square test of the Career Profile results (using the computational guide in Appendix A) revealed there was no relationship between the Career Profile score and success at AGLA. The chi-square analysis only revealed what the field managers already knew. In fact, the Career Profile had long since lost credibility, and field managers routinely were overruling the recommendation of the test.

Since the implementation of the computer interview at AGLA, over 40,000 potential agents have taken the interview and over 6,000 of those applicants have been hired. The value of this database to AGLA is without measure. Jim Tuerff, President of AGLA, said in a 1992 presentation to all managers, "The information we have gathered via the computer interview is one of the most valuable assets we have at AGLA."

AGLA now has the responses to 150 computer interview questions for each applicant. They have the sales and tenure results for each of the 6,000 hires. They have this information organized by region, district, and size of office. This allows AGLA to further refine the accuracy and utility of the validity studies produced by the computer interview.

Reflecting the fluid nature of selection criteria, AGLA has gone through five separate validity studies since the implementation of the computer interview. And, surprise, surprise, surprise, each of

129

the five validity studies has revealed new and changing predictive questions.

AGLA is now in the process of expanding the computer interview to conduct exit interviews of agents who terminate. Remember, people are more honest to a computer and thus are far more likely to reveal candid information to a computer exit interview as opposed to a human or paper-and-pencil counterpart. This exit interview will provide additional information for management to further understand and refine the employment procedures and qualifications.

Also, AGLA will begin using the computer to interview new agents approximately sixty days after they have been on the job. Research has shown that sixty days is a particularly vulnerable time for new hires. A computer interview at this time which is directed toward "How's it going on the new job" will reveal agents who are seriously considering termination. AGLA managers will be trained to talk to these agents and take action which will encourage the agent to remain on the payroll until the 'normal new job depression' passes. This data will also be used to develop an objective criterion validity model to predict the likelihood of termination just as Dr. John Greist constructed a model to predict the probability of a suicide attempt.

AGLA has clearly experienced positive results from the use of the computer-assisted employment interview. Why? Because they are now using a consistent structured employment interview for every agent applicant and they are using that information to develop and validate their own selection models. AGLA knows where their Stink, Mud, and Crystal Lakes are.

Go ahead, reward yourself. Enjoy a Reese's™ Peanut Butter Cup. Take advantage of the synergistic benefits derived from combining peanut butter (the biographical study) and chocolate (the structured job interview). I guarantee that your employee selection process will never operate better.

B. J. & Bubba
Cowboy Tips on Employee Selection

*You can't tell how good a
man or a watermelon is 'til
you thump 'em.*

CHAPTER TEN

OTHER COMPUTER INTERVIEWS

"A crooked tree will never straighten its branches."

You don't have to limit the application of the computer to the employment interview. You can put its tremendous power and capabilities to use in four other interview applications: the exit interview, the employee attitude survey, the promotion interview, and the morale interview.

The employee exit interview represents an excellent opportunity to gather meaningful data. Research has already proven that applicants are more honest in computer interview situations than in other interview methods. It only stands to reason that people leaving the firm should be even more honest. After all, what have they got to lose?

In fact, their anticipated honesty during an exit interview has been one of the main problems with traditional exit interviewing. Departing employees may feel a little gun shy about burning any bridges behind them. They may feel embarrassed about quitting the firm and have some reservations about bad mouthing their supervisors or the company. Likewise, the supervisors would rather endure a whipping than conduct a possibly confrontational exit interview and face up to their own shortcomings.

Simply put, the person-to-person exit interview is a poor and ineffective human resources procedure for gathering valuable information from departing employees, but the computer can be put to use gathering exit interview information in a consistent manner and without the fears of confrontation and retribution.

If companies truly strive to reduce employee turnover and retain the best employees, it makes good sense to determine why employees are leaving. Departing employee suggestions for improvement often prove beneficial in focusing efforts to improve the work place, for their responses to questions regarding pay, benefits, working conditions, supervisory capability, management competency, training programs, job responsibilities, etc. can help shape future employment policies and corporate culture. Exit interviews can also gather demographics such as age, shift, department, race, sex, length of service, and pay range which can be used as a basis for various management reports and analysis purposes.

Many retail companies have uncovered a lot of theft using computerized employee exit interviewing. They've asked employees, "Are you aware of theft within the company?" If the answer is yes, the computer then asks the logical follow-up question, "Would you be willing to talk about it?" They told the computer they would. The obvious question is, "Why didn't they come forward before and mention the instances of theft?" The answer is that they were never asked. The computer will ask those uncomfortable questions while a human will seek to avoid them.

Obviously, the computer can store exit interview responses in the same type of database constructed for the employment interview. This creates the opportunity for instant, complete, perpetual, and meaningful reports.

Many companies use the computer interview format to conduct perpetual employee attitude surveys. Each month they ask a given percentage of their employees to complete a computer interview. This strategy provides a significant database with plenty of good survey information for analysis. It also gives management immediate access to feedback from employees, which then allows them to deliver immediate attention to areas of concern.

The importance of job attitudes and their relationship to job performance has been the subject of numerous human resources research studies over the years. In a landmark study by Edward E. Lawler III and Lyman W. Porter, they investigated which factors determine the effort an employee puts into his or her job and which factors impact the relationship between the effort given and the ultimate performance achieved.

Lawler and Porter hypothesize that attitudes determine the amount of effort an employee puts into his or her job: the value of rewards and the probability that rewards depend upon effort. The underlying basis of the study is that rewards will be valued by the individual to the extent that he or she believes such rewards will provide satisfaction of security, esteem, social, self-actualization, autonomy, and other needs.

Lawler and Porter found that those beliefs are involved in determining effort. In order to modify behavior to desired performance levels, it is important to understand employee attitudes and those employees' perceptions of rewards and their ability to achieve them through performance.

The computer-generated employee attitude survey keeps management continually appraised of changes in these critical areas and how they can impact overall performance goals. Typically, attitude surveys take place annually or semi-annually and consist of voluminous questions regarding topics ranging from job categories to communications and from supervision to work hours and benefits. After this mass of data is gathered, the number crunchers churn out reams of reports purporting to uncover various attitudes and productivity relationships. Trying to digest all of this information proves impossible. Therefore, the next step in this corporate quagmire is to set up committees to study the problem and recommend potential solutions. Next, after endless meetings, either everybody involved in the process starts to lose interest or it's time to do it all over again, making the work accomplished to date useless or outdated.

Obviously, something is pitifully wrong with our attempts to assess employee attitudes. At Aspen Tree Software, we believe a simple and monthly attitude questionnaire can solve this dilemma. We subscribe to the method recommended by Dr. Scott Myers over twenty years ago in his Harvard Business Review article, "Conditions For Manager Motivation." Myers said that critical job satisfaction factors could be categorized into two sets of characteristics: maintenance factors (pay, working conditions, social factors, physical factors, and benefits) and motivational factors (growth, achievement, recognition, and responsibility). Furthermore, there was the overriding factor of the job itself. Using this information, we have developed a simple survey form that asks only a few questions about maintenance and motivational aspects of a job. Then we ask employees to respond to the big question, "Overall, how satisfied are you with your job?"

This survey is given to approximately ten percent of the employees in a work group every month and trends are measured and graphed. If the trend is positive, there is no need to take massive action. As the cowboys say, "Don't fix what ain't broke." However, if the trends deteriorate, it is time to take action and further investigate the job environment.

The bottom line in any corporate endeavor is productivity, and a direct correlation between employee attitudes and productivity has been proven by numerous research studies. Most administrators, however, would probably concede that their efforts to survey attitudes have more often than not proven to be a waste of time and energy.

The problem rests in the way employee survey data is accumulated. In plain English, the execution is faulty. People will provide straightforward answers to important questions if the survey is properly presented. In our experience, this is best accomplished by using brief on-line attitude surveys which are easy to use, interesting, and designed to guard confidentiality. Attitude assessment provides critical information the administrator cannot be without if he or she wants to maximize productivity and keep the best employees for the job, but more sophisticated data analysis techniques have worked to exacerbate the problem of trying to decipher and understand statistical information. Simply stated, administrators receive too much computer output, not too little. As a result, the important information gets lost in a forest of jargon, verbiage, and meaningless numbers. As M. R. Cooper (1982) aptly observed, "Some surveyors, both professional research firms and in-house groups, think that a survey is only as good as the amount of complex data it generates." In actuality, exactly the opposite is true: less is more.

Instead of letting modern technology overwhelm your operations, use computer power with discretion. Using computers to conduct employee surveys not only makes technological sense, it makes good business sense as well. R. Ferrara and R. N. Nolan (1974) esti-

135

mated that twenty to forty percent of the total cost of conducting an attitude survey stemmed from transferring paper-and-pencil interview data into a computer-acceptable form. In addition to being able to obtain more relevant information more timely and economically, once again computer interviewing results in more reliable information because people respond more honestly and candidly to computer-generated questions. People want to communicate openly, perceive confidentiality as a key ingredient in delivering honesty and candor, and view the automated computer survey as a way to achieving confidentiality.

The promotion interview represents a third type of computer interview. Just as you can interview someone via the computer for an initial job position within your firm, you can use the computer to interview him or her for a lateral transfer or a move up the corporate ladder. Here you will use a different set of interview questions developed to assess whether the particular employee is ready and qualified for promotion to a specific job.

Employees progress along their job careers at different paces. The computer-generated interview can help you assess which employees possess the experience, knowledge, skills, and desire to move on to the next job level. It can also help you single out which employees may need special training or development programs to best tap their underlying potential. Likewise, information generated in promotion interviews can help you assess weaknesses in your training and development programs which need to be addressed to better use the talents of your employees.

Use of the computer in promotion interviewing, just as it does in the initial hiring interview, helps eliminate any deep-seated biases. The computer interview process proceeds without prejudice, making sure you promote the best person for the job, helping to eliminate the opportunity for discrimination and EEOC complaints against your firm.

The geographical dispersion of many national and international companies makes promotion interviewing an interesting challenge. Use of the computer helps to ensure that each interviewee gets a fair shot at the job opening in the company. The computer also delivers tremendous travel, administration, and time savings since much of the interview process can take place over the phone or via interactive computers from multiple company locations. A logical extension of this process would be to combine the promotional computer interview with a computerized job posting system.

While computers help you hire the best people for the job during the initial hiring efforts, the use of computerized attitude surveys and computerized promotion interviews on a periodic basis keeps you focused on retaining your best people and promoting them into positions which best use their talents and satisfy their needs.

Finally, one of the most exciting uses of the computer interview is the sixty-day morale interview. Aspen Tree Software developed this interview based on research conducted by the Menninger Clinic in Topeka, Kansas, which developed from a serious problem encountered by the Peace Corps during the early days. Specifically, the Peace Corps was experiencing a devastatingly high attrition rate in the early days of service by its volunteers. The Corps had done an exhaustive job of training and counseling its volunteers to prepare them for the shock of service in a strange and often hostile environment, but nothing seemed to work, and volunteers were returning to America in the very early days of their service. The problem was so acute that the very existence of the Peace Corps was in jeopardy. Fortunately, the Peace Corps retained the services of the psychologists at the Menninger Clinic.

The Menninger psychologists noticed that most volunteers left in the first sixty days of service. They also noticed that once the sixty-day anniversary date had passed, there was a dramatic drop in the number of volunteers who resigned. This observation was discovered to be part of a rhythmic cycle (Figure 10-1) of anticipation, depression, normalcy, and re-entry. In spite of extensive counseling, volunteers would enter the Peace Corps service with a high level of anticipation and excitement. This emotion was soon followed by an unavoidable period of depression. Those volunteers who remained in service beyond the sixty-day mark soon moved out of their depression towards a more normal level of morale. This level of morale was maintained until the end of their service when some of the original excitement and anticipation returned. This cycle of events was labeled as the 'Morale Curve' by the psychologists.

Interestingly, the psychologists determined there was no cure for sixty-day depression other than time. Volunteers were told to expect this emotion and recognize it as a very normal part of their adjustment to foreign service. They were told to wait for another thirty days and it would almost always go away. The situation was hopeless, and normal. Amazingly, after this information was disseminated to the volunteers, the attrition rate dropped dramatically and the Peace Corps moved on to accomplish many of its objectives.

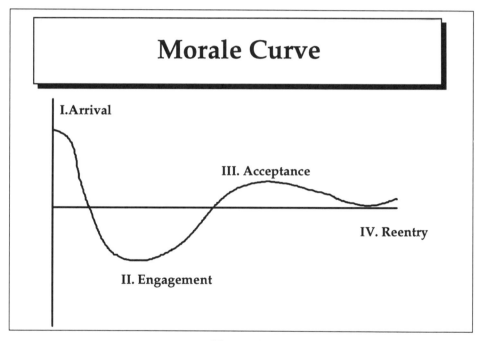

Figure 10-1

Eventually, the psychologists realized they had discovered a phenomenon that was not isolated to Peace Corps volunteers; they had defined a universal rhythm of life. They learned that almost any major change or event in a person's life will progress through the 'Morale Curve' sequence of emotions. In a way, this should not be surprising. Think how mothers often become depressed after the birth of a child, or remember how blue you became after your last vacation. The psychologists learned that even events as trivial as a movie or a party will progress through the 'Morale Curve' cycle.

Imagine the effect of a new job on the 'Morale Curve.' This would prompt, in most cases, a full manifestation of the cycle. Could this be a major contributor to the early termination results in many companies? I think so. Why not use a computer to conduct a 'Morale Curve' interview of all new employees and use the results to guide the supervisor through an educational interview with the depressed employee? And why not use the results of the morale interview to conduct a criterion validity study which satisfactorily predicts those employees most likely to be terminating? Such a statistical model would allow companies to have a two-tiered sieve to help in the selection and retention process. Profile 1 would be used for hiring and profile 2 would be used to solidify the success of the hiring decision.

Undoubtedly, there will be other interviews developed to take advantage of the benefits offered by the computer. Aspen Tree will be in the forefront of these advancements. By putting the power of the various computer interviews to work for your company, you will experience significant improvements in your employee selection and retention results.

B.J. & Bubba
Cowboy Tips on Employee Selection

An old-timer is a man who has a lot of
interesting experiences, some of 'em true.

Chapter Eleven

THE FUTURE

"Young liars turn into old thieves."

What lies ahead for advanced technology and the field of employee selection? In a word: video. I'm not talking about watching a VCR; I am talking about video generated from computer RAM. Given enough external memory, personal computers are now able to store and retrieve videos with the same ease as a section of text. This opens enormous possibilities. Consider the following study I conducted with one of my university classes.

I developed a typical paper-and-pencil question relating to attitudes about internal theft. I first asked my students to respond to the question, "What would you do if you saw a co-worker steal something?" There were four possible responses. Following are the percentages of student responses:

1. Report it to security or police	38%
2. Report it to my supervisor	52%
3. Talk to the employee who was stealing	8%
4. Think about it	2%

Figure 11-1

I waited for a month, then I showed them a five-second video of a female employee stealing something. I then asked the same students what they should do if they were co-workers of this woman

140

and had seen her steal. Following was the response pattern after the students saw the video:

1. Report it to security or police	21%
2. Report it to my supervisor	30%
3. Talk to the employee	30%
4. Think about it	19%

Figure 11-2

Notice the difference in response patterns between Figure 11-1 and Figure 11-2. There's clear evidence that people respond differently to seeing something happen than they do when they are merely asked to consider a possible situation.

Without a doubt, the future will be even more impacted by the computer as it develops bigger memory, more power and virtually unlimited capabilities.

Pushing along the development of interactive video capabilities, programs now being developed by Aspen Tree Software are so detailed that instead of asking a question, the computer software will show a video vignette of a specific circumstance that the applicant will be required to respond to. Our software will show a brief video from RAM illustrating a customer situation and ask the applicant to respond directly to a life-like drama.

Consider the video possibilities of the in-basket exercise, for example. A computer could be stocked with 500 or more different video vignettes and a person applying for a job or seeking a promotion would be required to go through this maze of video questions and situations relating to supervision, customer service, etc. The end result? A much clearer picture of the applicant's aptitude for the job.

Fiber optics make this even more exciting since all of this could be done via interactive video optic telephone equipment. The computer interviewing possibilities are very bright. As companies continue their downsizing, the move toward video computer interviewing via fiber optics will be accelerated.

I want to re-emphasize that the video capabilities I refer to are generated directly from the computer itself, not from an awkward and unwieldy external source.

Just as Aspen Tree Software now has thousands of computer interview questions, we will soon have equal numbers of video vignettes in our library covering situations such as supervisory decisions, customer service, employee performance, employee integrity, etc.

Video from RAM is the direction of computer interviewing, yet, even this breakthrough is not a pill. There are no quick fixes for effective interviewing techniques in the arena of employee selection for front-line positions, and there never will be.

I am always asked for a hiring tip. I have one and I have saved it for the last chapter. I hope you'll take the time to read it.

B.J. & Bubba
Cowboy Tips on Employee Selection

*A cowpoke who's been riding against the wind
knows the strength of it.*

Chapter Twelve
PULLING BULLS WITH JIM

"Do something you like and you'll never work a day in your life."

I am always asked for a tip about hiring. "There must be one thing you always look for in an employee," people say. This type of question is a vestige of the desire to find a selection pill. Remember, there aren't any. I have no divine secret that will solve all problems. When I am asked for a hiring tip, I avoid the question by re-emphasizing the absence of short cuts and the necessity of hard work. In spite of my reluctance to reveal a tip, I grant that there is one thing that I always look for in a prospective employee. I try to hire someone who is satisfied with his or her life in general and who specifically will like the work required by the job for which they are applying.

That's when I think of Jim Elliot, a Wyoming cowboy who is good at what he does because he loves it. I always remember Jim when students ask me, "What kind of career do you recommend for me when I graduate?" My answer is always the same, "Do something you like and you'll never work a day in your life." By that definition, Jim is the hardest worker I have ever met who has never worked. I had the great privilege of riding with Jim for a few days in the summer of 1989.

Jim is the manager of the Grizzley Ranch in the remote North Park Valley of northern Colorado. I met Jim one afternoon when I impulsively pulled off the highway and drove down a gravel road to a beautiful ranch compound I had seen. I had a few free days and thought it might be fun to ride with some real cowboys. Honestly, I didn't really think any genuine cowboys would let me ride with them, but they might let me fix fences or work in the hay fields. As I drove up, I saw some cowboys grooming horses at the corral and I quickly decided it took less courage to talk to them than it did to knock on the door of the large Victorian house in the middle of the compound.

All eyes were on me as I nervously stepped out of the car. A stranger was an exciting 'happening' at the ranch. I took a deep breath and consciously lowered my voice at least two octaves. "How do?" I drawled. My voice didn't crack; so far, so good. "Is the boss man around?" I tilted my head back and lowered my jaw. A tall red-bearded cowboy stepped forward and said, "Well, I'm the manager if that's what you mean. The name's Jim Elliot. What can I do for you?" The ball was in my court. I had to say something. "Uhhh, I'll work for free if you got anything for me to do. I'm a good hand." Jim stepped closer until his eyes were twelve inches away from mine. "You ever pull bulls, son?" I heard some cowboys giggle. "No, sir," I squeaked in a sound four octaves higher than my original voice. "Can you ride?" he continued as he lit a cigarette with a single stroke of his cupped hand and conspicuously blew the smoke out the side of his mouth. Jim had now clearly established that he was in charge of this conversation. "Sure, I can ride plenty good as long as the horse is arthritic, brain-damaged, and over twenty years old." With a slight smile he said, "Sounds good to me. Be here day after tomorrow at 6:00 A.M.; we're gonna let you pull some bulls."

Pull bulls? What the hell is pulling bulls? It didn't matter as I drove away from the ranch. All I knew was that I was going to be a real cowboy on a real working ranch. "Hot damn!"

I drove directly to the Longhorn Saddle shop in Laramie and bought a pair of chaps and some silver spurs from Andy Hysong, the owner and master saddle maker. I had Andy put conchos on the chaps and stitch "Bubba" across the top. I also purchased a set of leather saddle bags to match the chaps. I already had a duster and a pair of boots, so I was now totally equipped to be a cowboy.

Andy was curious and asked me what I was going to do with all this new gear. I proudly told him I was going to help some cowboys pull some bulls. "You're gonna pull bulls?" Andy chuckled.

"Do you have any idea what you're gettin' into?" "Nope, but I think I'm up to it." I was getting nervous.

Next, I drove to Corral West, the local western store to buy a pair of Wells Lamont leather gloves that I heard Paul Harvey talk about on the radio. I knew that you could only buy Wells Lamont gloves at the best western stores. Corral West didn't have any and suggested I try Safeway. I found the gloves there between the diapers and the paper plates. What a let-down.

I asked several people if they knew what pulling bulls was all about. Nobody seemed to know for sure, but one person told me, "I think when it happens you will hear the saddest sound in the world." That worried me and I began suspecting the worst. I wasn't sure I could do that to any living male creature, but I was committed now and I had to go through with it.

Sleep was a rare commodity for the next two days. I was simultaneously excited and distressed. Could I pull a bull? Would I waver at the last moment and drop the pulling instrument? Finally, it was time to go and I headed for the Grizzley ranch. I stopped at the nearest convenience store and bought some bananas and a chicken salad sandwich for lunch.

The drive to the ranch was perfect. I saw the sun rise over the mountains just as a morning rain released the scent of the sagebrush. A flock of geese flew in front of me and added sound to the moment. It was intoxicating. I was on my way to be a cowboy. At that moment, life was perfectly balanced.

When I pulled into the ranch, the horses were already saddled. "Thank God for small favors." I saw movement and lights in the house, so I put on my chaps and spurs and walked in to join the cowboys for a cup of coffee. As I swaggered into the kitchen, I wasn't sure if I should have my spurs on in the kitchen or not. A breach of protocol could seriously damage any shred of credibility I might have had. My relief was immense as I saw spurs on the other cowboys.

We had coffee (sans Jack Daniels) and made plans for the day. There was Jim, four other cowboys, and myself. It was simple, the six of us pokes would take three trucks and livestock trailers fifteen miles to the north of the ranch and pull the bulls. When we were finished, three cowboys would drive the trucks (loaded with the recently pulled bulls) back to the ranch corral and the rest of us would ride back to the ranch bringing the extra horses with us.

We arrived at an immense range at about 7:00 A.M. and began building a temporary corral to put the bulls in. By now I had learned that pulling bulls was the cowboy term for separating them from the heifers they had been spending the spring with. The bulls ('hang downs' as Jim called them) had been doing their job 'pregging' the ladies and now it was time to leave them alone. My relief was overwhelming; I wasn't going to have to hurt these hang downs with whom I felt some primitive identification.

There were eighteen hang downs that needed pulling. We divided ourselves into three groups and rode in different directions to find the quarry and drive them back to the corral.

I carefully placed my sandwich and banana in the thin leather saddle bags on the back of a horse named Chubb and rode off to the west with Jim. Sometimes you just know when a person is a pro. That's how Jim was. He was totally in harmony with his calling as a cowboy. It was the way he rode, the way he gave orders to the cowboys, the way he respectfully treated the horses, and most importantly, the way he was aware of my fear of feeling insignificant in the events to come.

Jim is a third generation cowboy who learned his craft in southern Wyoming. I had already known from the other cowboys that Jim

146

was considered to be the best in the business and it was an honor to ride with him. Todd Krenning, a twenty-nine year-old cowboy from Cody, Wyoming, told me, "I grew up on a ranch and been cowboying full time now for over eleven years and I still don't know half of what Jim does. I learn something new every time I ride with him." Jim was the best in the West and I was riding alone with him for the next five hours.

Jim's wisdom was boundless. He could look at a gate and state with 100% confidence, "Pete was the last person to go through here." I was astounded. "How the hell do you know that?" My jaw was gaping. Jim responded, "Nobody else wraps the chain to lock the gate like Pete does. Everybody does it slightly different."

I learned it was going to snow five feet in the winter because the skunk cabbage always grew just enough to keep their heads a foot above the snow and they were six feet tall.

Jim could ride to the top of a ridge and see a herd a mile in the distance with 200 cows and instantly determine the number of bulls that we had to pull. Once, I started to ride Chubb across a marshy bog. Jim saw what I was about to do and quickly grabbed Chubb's rein to stop him. "Son," he said, "Don't take that horse down there. If that mud's deep, he'll get stuck and we got a problem." "Sure," I responded, "but, how do we get to the other side?" Jim released the rein and pointed to a large heifer a few feet away. "Just drive that white face through the mud. If she makes it, so can we." Wisdom!

We crossed the bog and Jim located a heifer who was still in heat. He separated her from the herd and moved her towards the temporary corral. The hang downs feeling a need to do their job simply followed her. More wisdom! Things don't have to be complicated.

Soon it was high noon and eighty-five degrees. I had been in the saddle for over five hours. By now I knew a cow horse had four speeds. Speed one is a slow walk. I can handle that. Speed three is a smooth rhythmic gait. That speed scared me, but as long as I hung on, I was alright. Speed four is when the horse runs as fast as he can. Thankfully, Chubb never tested me with speed four, but I saw Jim ride that fast on several occasions while he roped a calf. But, what about speed two? Unfortunately, that was Chubb's speed ninety percent of the time. It's what I call the jackhammer speed. In that mode, no two of Chubb's hoofs ever touched the earth at the same time. The net effect of this was a relentless jackhammer trot which flung me straight up and down for almost five hours. I don't think I need to emphasize that this is not a pleasant experience for a normal male.

I survived and finally arrived with the bulls at the corral we had assembled earlier in the morning. It was lunch time. Jim and the other cowboys dismounted and retrieved their lunches from igloo coolers in the trucks. I reached into my saddle bags and felt a sensation which can best be described as warm oatmeal. The combination of thirty miles at speed two, thin leather saddle bags, and eighty-five degrees had not been positive for my chicken salad sandwich and two bananas. Much to the amusement of everyone, I ate it anyway. Other than walnuts, I can't imagine any edible substance which could survive those conditions.

Finally, the bulls were loaded into the three trailers. Jim and two other cowboys drove them to a new range while the rest of us led the horses back to the ranch. We had fifteen miles to go, but I was numb and it didn't matter. Besides, I was getting the hang of things. And, best of all, we would all end the day back at the ranch bonding and reliving the pull while the sun set over the aspen trees. My semi-coherent mind pictured a galvanized water tank filled with at least 100 long necks symmetrically protruding through clear chipped ice. It would be a perfect ending to the day.

When we were a mile from the ranch, Todd pulled up next to me and stated, "I sure am thirsty." "Yeah, me too." I began to get excited. Todd continued, "Miss Judy makes the best iced tea in Colorado." My heart jumped to my throat and my voice cracked as I wailed, "Iced tea? You mean we're gonna drink iced tea?" "You bet," Todd smiled. "Judy lets the tea sit in the sun all day and you can't drink anything better than that after a day of riding in the sun." "Are you sure?" I whimpered with moist eyes.

We met Jim and his crew and drank the tea. Actually, Todd was right; it was the best I ever drank. Yet its hard to imagine cowboys sitting around the bunk house, hoisting a glass of Lipton's to the rafters and saying, "Guys, it doesn't get any better than this."

After about thirty minutes, the cowboys left to be with their families. I was kind of hoping to ride into town with them and raise a little hell. It just didn't happen that way. But I must have done something right because Todd asked me to ride the high country with him to pick up strays. And I was honored when Jim said he would be pleased to have me ride with him on the cattle drive next month.

It was a perfect day and the beginning of a friendship between Jim and me. I knew I was lucky to have been in the presence of a gifted individual. Jim is the best at what he does and he's the best because he loves his occupation. I remember him telling me: "I'm a cowboy because I don't want to do anything else." Bet on cowboys, not horses. I'd bet on Jim anytime.

B.J. and Bubba
Cowboy Tips on Employee Selection

The wildest broncos were always rode someplace else.

BIBLIOGRAPHY

Asher, J.J., "The Biographical Item: Can It Be Improved?," *Personnel Psychology*, No. 25, 1972.

Barrett, Richard, "Guide to Using Psychological Tests," *Harvard Business Review*, 41, September-October, 1963.

Bass, B.M., "Further Evidence on the Dynamic Character of Criteria," *Personnel Psychology*, 15, 1962.

Blum, Milton L., and James C. Naylor, *Industrial Psychology: Its Theoretical and Social Foundations*, New York, Harper & Row, 1968.

Brown, Steven, "Long-Term Validity of a Personal History Item Scoring Procedure," *Journal of Applied Psychology*, Vol. 63, No. 6, 1978.

Carlson, Robert, Paul Thayer, Eugene Mayfield, and Donald Peterson, "Improvements in the Selection Interview," *Personnel Journal*, Vol. 50, No. 4, 1971.

Cascio, Wayne, "Accuracy of Verifiable Biographical Information Blank Responses," *Journal of Applied Psychology*, No. 60, 1975.

Childs, Auralee, and Richard J. Klimoski, "Successfully Predicting Career Success: An Application of the Biographical Inventory," *Journal of Applied Psychology*, Vol. 71, No. 1, 1986.

Cooper, M.R., "Traditional Employee Attitude Surveys Don't Work," *Management Review*, August, 1982.

Dipboye, Robert, "Self-fulfilling Prophecies in the Selection Recruitment Interview," *Academy of Management Review*, Vol. 7, No. 4, 1982.

England, George W., *Development and Use of Weighted Application Blanks*, Industrial Relations Center, Minneapolis, University of Minnesota, 1971.

Engler-Parish, Pat, *The Employment Screening Interview: A Relational Control Analysis*, Master's Thesis, University of Wyoming, 1987.

Ferrara, R., and R. N. Nolan, "New Look at Computer Data Entry," In W. C. House (Ed.), *Data Base Management*, Petrocelli Books, New York, 1974.

Fleishman, Edwin, and Joseph Berniger, "Using the Application Blank to Reduce Office Turnover," *Personnel*, Vol. 37, 1960.

Florence, P. S., *Economics of Fatigue and Unrest and the Efficiency of Labor in the English and American Industry*, Henry Holt & Co., New York, 1924.

Greist, John, Dr., and Paulette Selmy, "Computer Administered Cognitive

Behavioral Therapy for Depression, *"The American Journal of Psychiatry,* Vol. 1, January, 1990.

Guthrie, Edwin R., "Personality in Terms of Associative Learning," *Personality and the Behavior Disorders,* edited by Joseph M. Hund, New York, The Ronald Press Co., 1944.

Herzberg, Fredrick, *The Motivation to Work,* John Wiley & Sons, 1959.

Hollinger, Richard, *Theft By Employees,* Lexington Press, 1988.

Janz, T., "Initial Comparisons of Patterned Behavior Description Interviews Versus Unstructured Interviews," *Journal of Applied Psychology,* 67, 1982.

Johnson, Doug, Nancy Newton, and Leon Peek, "Predicting Tenure of Municipal Clerical Employees: A Multiple Regression Analysis," Public Personnel Management, 1979.

Lawrence, Daniel G., Barbara L. Salsburg, John G. Dawson, and Zachary D. Fasman, "Design and Use of Weighted Application Blanks," *Personnel Administrator,* March, 1982.

Lawler, Edward E. III, and Lyman W. Porter "Antecedent Attitudes of Effective Managerial Performance", *Organizational Behavior and Human Performance 2,* 1967.

Martin, Christopher L., and Dennis H. Nagao, "Some Effects of Computerized Interviewing on Job Applicant Responses, *Journal of Applied Psychology,* Vol. 74, No. 1, 1989.

Menninger, Walter, *The Meaning of Morale,* The Menninger Foundation, 1969.

Mitchell, Brooks, *Three-Year Weighted Blank Criterion Study to Predict Tenure,* Doctoral Dissertation, North Texas State University, 1986.

Myers, Scott, "Conditions for Manager Motivation," *Harvard Business Review,* 1966.

____, *Every Employee a Manager,* University Association, 1990.

Owens, W. A., Background data in M. D. Dunnette (Ed.), *Handbook of Industrial and Organizational Psychology,* Chicago, Rand McNally, 1976.

Roach, Darrell, "Double-Cross Validation of a Weighted Application Blank Over Time," *Journal of Applied Psychology,* Vol. 55, 1971.

Rosenbaum, Richard, "Development of a "Weighted Application Blank to Predict Theft," *Journal of Applied Psychology,* Vol. 61, 1976.

Scanlon, Joseph, (F. G. Lesieur and E. S. Puckett), "The Scanlon Plan Has Proved Itself," *Harvard Business Review,* No. 47, 1969.

Schmidt, Frank L., and Leon B. Kaplan, "Composite vs. Multiple Criteria: A Review and Resolution of the Controversy," *Personnel Psychology* 24, 1971.

Schneider, B., "Organizational Climates," an essay, *Personnel Psychology*, Vol. 28, 1975.

Schuh, Alan, "Application Blank Items and Intelligence as Predictors of Turnover," *Personnel Psychology*, 20 (Spring,) 1967.

____, "Contrast Effect in the Employment Interview," *Bulletin of the Psychonomic Society*, 1978.

Shott, G. L., L. E. Albright, and J. R. Glennon, "Predicting Turnover in an Automated Office Situation, *Personnel Psychology*, 16 (Autumn,) 1963.

Smith, Patricia Cain, "The Prediction of Individual Differences in Susceptibility to Industrial Monotony," *Journal of Applied Psychology*, Vol. 39, No. 5, 1955.

Stuit, D. B., and J. T. Wilson, "The Effect of an Increasingly Well Defined Criterion on the Prediction of Success at Naval Training School (Tactical Radar), *Journal of Psychology*, 30, 1946.

Tucker, D. H., and P. M. Rowe, "Relationship Between Expectancy and Casual Attributions, and Final Hiring Decisions in the Employment Interview," *Journal of Applied Psychology*, Vol. 64, 1979.

Wernimont, P., "Re-evaluation of a Weighted Application Blank for Office Personnel," *Journal of Applied Psychology*, 46 (December,) 1962.

Wiesner, Willi H., and Steven F. Cronshaw, "A Meta-Analytic Investigation of the Impact of Interview Format and Degree of Structure on the Validity of the Employment Interview," *Journal of Occupational Psychology*, Vol. 61, 1988.

APPENDIX A

HOW TO TELL IF YOUR SELECTION PROCEDURES (TESTS) ARE WORKING

Using the following computing guide, you can conduct a chi-square analysis to determine if your selection procedures or tests actually predict (at a statistically significant level) a specific criterion.

EXAMPLE: You are using a fifteen-point test to predict employee turnover. A score of eight or more is used as a passing score and an applicant who scores seven or less fails the test. Short tenure is determined to be an employee who terminates in the first six months of employment and long tenure is an employee who completes more than six months. The first step is to hire a minimum of twenty-five applicants (See Table 1.) who pass the test and twenty-five who fail the test. Now you have to wait six months to see who terminates and who remains on the job. When you know this data the results can be arranged in a 2x2 table as illustrated in Table 1.

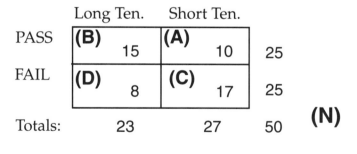

Table 1

In the above example, twenty-three employees achieved long tenure and twenty-seven were short tenure. Fifteen of the twenty-three long-tenure employees passed the test and seventeen of the short-tenure employees failed the test. Now use the following formula to compute chi-square for the above results.

$$\text{Chi-square} = \frac{N(AD-BC^2)}{(A+B)\ (C+D)\ (A+C)\ (B+D)}$$

OR

$$\frac{50\ [(10)\ (8)-(15)(17)]^2}{(25)\ (25)\ (27)\ (23)} = \frac{1,531,250}{388,125} \quad 3.94$$

Any number greater than 3.84 indicates (in accordance with EEOC recommendations) that there is at least a .05 level of significance. A significance level of .05 means that there are five chances in 100 that the results could have occurred randomly. Since the above calculation is greater than 3.84, the test can be said to be predicting tenure. A small number would indicate an increasing likelihood that the results occurred by chance and your selection procedure is probably not working. Obviously, the above computational guide could be used for other purposes such as disparate impact, training pass rates, etc.

THE GREENTREE™ COMPUTER-ASSISTED EMPLOYMENT INTERVIEW

Summary of Rationale, Methodology
and Legal Implications in Accordance with:

• *TITLE 7 OF THE 1964 CIVIL RIGHTS ACT*

• *1978 UNIFORM EMPLOYEE SELECTION GUIDE-LINES*

• *1990 AMERICAN WITH DISABILITIES ACT*

• *1991 CIVIL RIGHTS ACT*

The following dicussion and independent legal opinion provide information regarding the Greentree™ Computer-Assisted Employment Interview, which combines a structured job interview with continuous validity verification and the use of a computer. The document is written for those who need to understand the rationale behind the Greentree™ Interview as well as the possible legal ramifications of using a computer interview system vis-a-vis federal anti-discriminatory legislation.

INTRODUCTION

The Greentree™ Computer-Assisted Employment Interview (GCEI) is a computer-based pre-employment interview software program developed by Aspen Tree Software, Inc. (ATS) in response to the need for a better way to find competent, productive employees and to predict employee performance, customer service and turnover than with the traditional pencil and paper job application blank.

By using the speed and memory capacity of a computer system, the GCEI is able to compare information from the job applicants with a statistical profile of a highly successful, long-term employee for a particular company. This allows the employer to be more precise in finding the right person for any position vacancy.

Benefits of Computer Interviewing

One of the primary benefits of using a computer for job interviews is that the errors made by inexperienced interviewers are avoided. The computer never shows fatigue, never varies the emphasis with which a question is asked, and never judges the potential employee on the basis of such things as personal appearance.

Though it could never take the place of a face-to-face interview, the use of the GCEI as a pre-employment interview allows the employer to completely screen all potential applicants, thus saving interview time. Additionally, because of the ease with which data can be manipulated, the GCEI can probe each applicant's answers and ask follow-up questions. This provides a base of information that can be used by employers to select solid, qualified candidates even from among those who, for one reason or another, might normally fall to the low end of the desirability scale.

Summary of Rationale

The following discussion provides a careful look at the rationale behind the GCEI and the process by which it is gradually woven into the overall fabric of a company's hiring techniques.

The discussion begins with a brief section examining the rationale behind the GCEI, followed by an outline of its three primary features. The first of the appendices that follow the discussion provides answers to a series of commonly-asked questions regarding validity and adverse impact as they relate to the GCEI. The second appendix reproduces two letters presenting the independent legal opinion of Millisor & Nobil, a law firm specializing in employment law, which show that computer-assisted interviewing techniques in general have remained free from legal challenge based on *Title 7 of the 1964 Civil Rights Act, the 1978 Uniform Guidelines on Employee Selection*, the *1990 Americans With Disabilities Act*, and the *1991 Civil Rights Act*. In fact, because the GCEI is so carefully structured, repeatedly revised, and consistently administered, the attorneys' opinion is that the use of GCEI actually provides considerable protection for companies if the legality of their hiring processes is ever challenged.

The Greentree™ Computer-Assisted Employment Interview

The GCEI, developed by Aspen Tree Software, Inc., provides a structured job interview and perpetual validity studies tailored to fit specific companies and job types. It also allows for the use of computers to consistently administer pre-employment job interviews and gather data to be used to increase the value of the program for a specific company. The advantages of structure, on-going validity studies, and the use of computers in employee selection have all been demonstrated by credible and responsible research literature in the field, as well as by practical experience. Additionally, the GCEI, in combining the three, synergistically enhances the advantages. Figure 1 summarizes the elements that form the core of the GCEI.

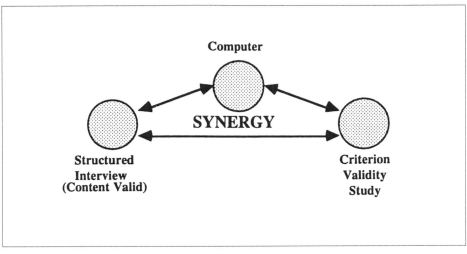

Figure 1

The Structured Job Interview

The GCEI's philosophy of employee selection is that there is no substitute for a structured job interview administered by the hiring manager. This belief is well substantiated in respected, juried personnel journals. A recent article based on over 150 controlled interview studies and published in the *Journal of Occupation Psychology* states:

> "The prediction for a difference by interview type was strongly supported. . . . [T]he unstructured interview proved to have the least predictive validity of all interview types. . . . [T]he structured interviews had mean validity coefficients twice those of unstructured interviews."

Validity

The validation of a selection procedure is very important to personnel management for it provides solid justification for any employment decision made. There are two types of validity related to employment interviews, content validity and criterion validity. Content validity requires that, as a whole, the questions asked during an interview relate to the knowledge, aptitudes, and other characteristics necessary to perform the work that the job requires. Criterion validity relates to an empirical or numerical weighting of certain questions which can be used to predict the probability of certain outcomes such as employee performance or longevity. The *Uniform Guidelines on Employee Selection of 1978* (UGES) require evidence of validation of a selection procedure when it adversely affects any employment opportunities (such as hire, transfer, or promotion) of a race, sex, or ethnic group.

The GCEI uses logic and company-specific information to provide content validity for the pre-employment job interview questions. Prior to a criterion-based validity study, the GCEI is not scored. It is used only as a guide for managers to interview serious applicants consistently and thoroughly. Using all information available, the manager, not the computer interview, decides the suitability of the applicant for employment.

The GCEI is both content and criterion valid. Aspen Tree Software methodology is consistent with the UGES as well as the guidelines recommended by the American Psychological Association publication *Guidelines for Use, Administration, and Development of Employee Tests.*

Content Validity

The UGES defines content validity as "data showing that a selection procedure is a representative sample of important work behaviors to be performed on the job." ATS uses content validity methodology to develop the original computer-aided interview (CAI) questions which relate to knowledge, skills, and other characteristics and abilities necessary to perform a job. An interview question is content valid if the applicants' responses could have a bearing on their demonstrated ability to perform the job satisfactorily. Asking secretarial applicants about the level of their typing skill would be considered a content valid question.

ATS believes that many areas of inquiry legitimately fit within the UGES definition of content validity. For example, in public contact jobs, we feel it is content valid to ask questions about the candidate's experience and attitudes relating to customer contact. Or, for outside sales jobs, it is within the UGES parameters to ask questions about personal networking to determine the potential sales leads the applicant may have.

160

Typical sources for content valid questions are job analyses, job descriptions, managerial focus groups, and outside expert opinions. Data from these sources are woven into the ATS software program in a manner that allows every applicant to be interviewed consistently by all interviewers. In some cases, ATS includes biographical questions in the GCEI which are not job related. The biographical responses are not given to the interviewer but are stored in the computer for future criterion validity analysis. If they are statistically demonstrated to be related to success on the job, they are later included in an interviewer's printout.

Criterion Validity

The UGES defines criterion validity as "empirical data showing that the selection procedure is predictive of or significantly correlated with important elements of work behavior." Furthermore, "criteria also may consist of measures other than work proficiency including, but not limited to, production rate, error rate, tardiness, absenteeism, and length of service, which may be used without a full job analysis if the user can show the importance of the criteria."

After all of the pre-employment interviews are complete, ATS collects the applicant responses to the GCEI and conducts a job family criterion study as recommended by Dr. George England in *Development and Use of Weighted Application Blanks*. A minimum of seventy-five applications that compare favorably to past successful hires in the same job family are placed in a "high criterion group," and the same number of applications that correlate to past unsuccessful hires are placed in a "low criterion group," as shown in Figure 2.

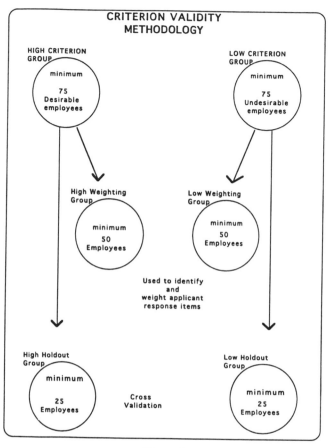

Figure 2

From each of these groups fifty applications are taken and are placed into high and low weighting groups. The remaining applications are placed into two holdout groups to be used as needed for more information. The responses on the high and low weighting group applications are then used to develop a scored profile which statistically mirrors the employer's past successful hires. This score allows the organization to efficiently screen in those job applicants who have the highest probability of success for each specific job family regardless of whether their overall application shows them to be potentially good, marginal, or poor employees. Figure 3 graphically demonstrates how this profile can be used to predict the number of good hires possible from each general category of applications.

Since this profile will change as new employees are added, ATS continues to monitor the GCEI and to readjust (and thereby revalidate) the profile as it changes. This process fully acknowledges and allows for the fact that selection criteria are fluid, not static.

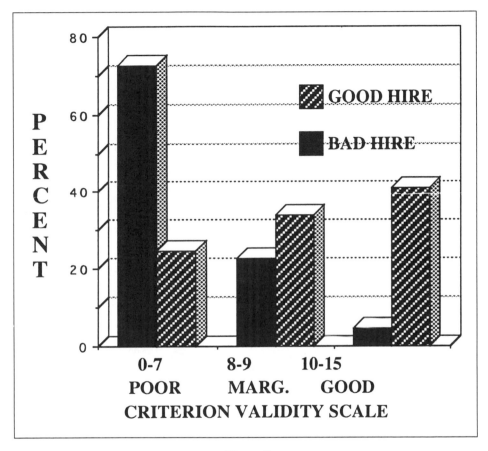

Figure 3
From Development and Use of Weighted Application Blanks by George England, 1971, Industrial Relations Center, University of Minnesota: Minneapolis, Minnesota.

The Computer-Based Structured Job Interview

Administering pre-employment interviews is an appropriate use for computers because they can gather information far more quickly than their human counterparts, and, with effectively written software, are more accurate and consistent as well. The GCEI allows for consistency, thoroughness, depth, and accuracy in the pre-interview procedure by using company-specific information and information from the occupational area in writing the questions for the preliminary structured job interview. Computers are also effective for use in interviews because, first, storage of information gathered during the GCEI is limited only by the capability of the user's computer system. Second, as studies conducted by ATS as well as by Duke University, Georgia Technical University, and the University of Wisconsin show, people prefer giving information to a computer (particularly, sensitive information) and are more likely to respond honestly to the computer as opposed to either a human interviewer or a pencil-and-paper interview.

Computers are especially effective for storing and retrieving information important in meeting EEOC and ADA guidelines. The GCEI collects information on an applicant's race, gender, and disability status, which can then be sorted on the basis of the pass/fail rates established by the criterion validity discussed above. This information is also important because companies are obliged to maintain evidence indicating the impact which their selection processes have on identifiable race, sex, or ethnic groups. Ease of manipulation and retrieval of data allows a company to easily demonstrate compliance with, for instance, the *Uniform Employee Selection Guideline's* adverse impact requirement, which states that any racial, ethnic, or sex group must be within 80% of the rate for the group with the highest interview scores.

Summary

The Greentree™ Computer-Assisted Employment Interview synergistically combines a structured job interview, verification of interview validity, and the use of the computer. The responses to the GCEI provide information for the perpetual analyses which are used to refine the program. Additionally, the GCEI provides an effective safeguard in meeting federal employment guidelines, because the criteria can be analyzed for fairness to any ethnic, racial, or sex group. The following letter discusses in detail the legal ramification of using the GCEI vis-a-vis federal Equal Employment Opportunity Commission anti-discriminatory restrictions.

APPENDIX A:

Questions Relating to Validity and Adverse Impact

The following section contains answers to questions that the reader may have concerning validity and adverse impact as they relate to the Greentree™ Computer-Assisted Employment Interview. These questions and answers are quoted directly from the *1978 Uniform Guidelines on Employee Selection*.

Q. Does the UGES require that only validated selection procedures be used?

A. *"No. Although validation of selection procedures is desirable in personnel management, the UGES requires users to produce evidence of validity only when the selection procedure adversely affects the opportunities of a race, sex, or ethnic group for hire, transfer, promotion, retention or other employment decision. If there is no adverse impact, there is no validation required under the Guidelines."*

Q. What is meant by adverse impact?

A. *"A selection rate for any racial, ethnic or sex group which is less than four-fifths (80%) of the rate for the group with the highest rate will generally be regarded by the federal enforcement agencies as evidence of adverse impact."*

Q. Are companies obliged to keep records which show whether its selection processes have an adverse impact?

A. *"Yes, under the Guidelines users are obliged to maintain evidence indicating the impact which their selection processes have on identifiable race, sex, or ethnic groups."*

Q. Is adverse impact determined on the basis of the overall selection process or for the components in that process?

A. *"Adverse impact is determined first for the overall selection process for each job. If there is no adverse impact for the overall selection process, in most circumstances there is no obligation under the Guidelines to investigate adverse impact for the components, or to validate the selection procedures for that job. And federal agencies generally will not take enforcement action based upon adverse impact of any component of the total selection process, including the separate parts of a multi-part selection procedure."*

Q. What is meant by "the total selection process"?

A. *"The total selection process refers to the combined effect of all selection procedures leading to the final employment decision such as hiring or promotion."*

APPENDIX B:

Legal Opinion

The following letters present the independent legal opinion of Millisor & Nobil, a law firm that specializes in employment law. The first letter responds to our request for a discussion of *Title 7 of the 1964 Civil Rights Act*, the *1978 Uniform Guidelines on Employee Selection*, the *1990 Americans With Disabilities Act*, and the *1991 Civil Rights Act* as they relate to the Greentree™ Computer-Assisted Employment Interview (GCEI). The second letter discusses the GCEI in light of the *1990 Americans With Disabilities Act, the 1991 Civil Rights Act*, and the *1978 Uniform Guidelines on Employee Selection*.

MILLISOR & NOBIL – A LEGAL PROFESSIONAL ASSOCIATION

November 15, 1991

Dr. Brooks Mitchell
ASPEN TREE SOFTWARE, INC.
1159 Granito
Laramie, Wyoming 82070

RE: The Greentree Computer-Assisted Employment Interview

Dear Dr. Mitchell:

You have requested our firm to review the Greentree™ Computer-Assisted Employment Interview (GCEI) developed by Aspen Tree Software, Inc., with an eye towards potential or real employment-related legal concerns. More specifically, you have asked us to evaluate the process in relation to existing anti-discrimination laws, whether on the federal or local level. Because there are some unique state laws, our opinion does not address those specifically. Our comments and conclusions here are thus limited to the overall methods of GCEI, and its resulting by-products.

Computer-assisted interviewing, in and of itself, does not run afoul of any federal statutes. Nor are we aware of any state statutes which directly seek to ban or even regulate computer interviewing. Indeed, our research as of this date has not unearthed a single case where computer interviewing was called into question.

With respect to EEO-type concerns relating to particular questions which may be posed by a developed GCEI, the federal Equal Employment Opportunity Commission - the administrative agency charged with primary responsibility for interpreting and ensuring compliance with both Title VII of the *1964 Civil Rights Act* and the federal *Age Discrimination in Employment Act* (ADEA)-has currently embraced the position that..."in most circumstances" there is no obligation to investigate adverse impact for the components of a selection process if the overall process does not produce a discriminatory impact. Simply stated, if a tailored GCEI does not, in fact, produce adverse impact on the whole, the EEOC will not scrutinize individual interview questions.

While virtually all states purport to interpret their discrimination laws in conformity with the federal counterparts, many have not hesitated to make use of their authority to provide protections over and above that provided by the federal legislation. Both Title VII and the ADEA were expressly enacted as "floors" rather than "ceilings" against unlawful discrimination. To the extent states or local governments would choose to attack individual questions within a GCEI, they remain free to do so. This is true whether or not the individual questions produce a net adverse impact. Of course, given the flexibility of the GCEI, individual questions can be screened by the user to minimize the chance that a local agency would find them objectionable.

The *1990 Americans with Disabilities Act* ("ADA") does, to a limited degree, regulate the questions which may be posed in a pre-employment interviewing process such as GCEI. For example, the EEOC's substantive regulations issued in accordance with its rule-making responsibilities under the Act state that "...an employer may not inquire about an individual's worker's compensation history at the pre-offer stage." 29 C.F.R. § 2630.13 (a) (1991). Nevertheless, pre-employment inquiries that solicit whether an applicant possesses the skill, experience, education and other job-related requirements for a position of employment are not prohibited. Under ADA regulations, an applicant with an "impairment," and therefore one who is "disabled" does not include someone who has "...a characteristic predisposition to illness or disease." 29 C.F.R. § 1630.2 (h). Further, the ADA does not altogether ban or even regulate all non job-related pre-employment inquiries. "[A] selection criterion that is not job-related and consistent with business necessity violates this section only when it screens out an individual with a disability (or a class of individuals with disabilities) on the basis of disability." 29 C.F.R. § 2630.10. You should also be aware that the ADA requires not only reasonable accommodation for the disabled applicant or employee at work, but in pre-employment testing processes as well. The GCEI method would thus have to be altered in those narrow circumstances where an applicant possessing a disability alerts an employer to the need for an alternative testing format or other testing accommodation due to his or her disability. 29 C.F.R. § 1630.11.

As designed, and if properly administered by Aspen Tree Software clientele, the GCEI should place the user in a distinct advantage for purposes of defending EEO challenges. The process appears to have built-in checks and balances that are designed to more swiftly (and perhaps even more accurately) "red flag" selection procedures producing an unlawful discriminatory impact. It has been our firm's general experience over the years that in most instances where simple structured or unstructured interviewing is employed, this very critical analysis is but an afterthought, undertaken only after a particular court action is commenced. Unfortunately, at that point the damage has already been done and the class of plaintiffs subject to potential equitable or legal relief is greatest. Moreover, because the GCEI is repeatedly revised to ensure content validity of the individual questions, the historical data supporting its continued use is both current and less speculative than other selection processes. Finally, the GCEI provides employers with complete documentation and a readily accessible source of records-obligations imposed (but not frequently ignored) by regulations promulgated under both Title VII and the ADEA. All in all, the GCEI affords employers with many readily apparent advantages over unstructured employment interviewing without, in and of itself, generating *any* identifiable "disadvantages."

We hope we have adequately addressed, in the abstract, the employed-related questions which may arise by virtue of your continued use of the GCEI. We would be more than happy to follow up on any specific concerns through the application and use of the GCEI. If you have any questions on the above, please do not hesitate to call at your earliest convenience.

Very truly yours,
Keith L. Pryatel
Douglas B. Brown

9150 SOUTH HILLS BOULEVARD • CLEVELAND, OHIO 44147-3599
CLEVELAND (216) 838-8800 • AKRON (216) 253-5500
TELEFAX (216) 838-8805

MILLISOR & NOBIL – A LEGAL PROFESSIONAL ASSOCIATION

January 3, 1992

Dr. Brooks Mitchell
ASPEN TREE SOFTWARE, INC.
1159 Granito
Laramie, Wyoming 82070

> RE: Continued Applicability of the Uniform Guidelines on Employee Selection in Light of The Americans With Disabilities Act and The Civil Rights Act of 1991

Dear Dr. Mitchell:

In response to your inquiry as to the continuing applicability of the *Uniform Guidelines on Employee Selection* (UGES) in light of passage of the *Americans With Disabilities Act* (ADA) and the *Civil Rights Act of 1991* (CRA '91), we offer the following. Your question is one of "first impression for us given the recency of these enactments. Furthermore, the EEOC has not yet established interpretive regulations under the CRA '91. Accordingly, our answer is based on our interpretation of the law and without the benefit of any courts having considered the precise question. As such, what we offer is an educated opinion as to how a court, confronted with the question, would respond.

The UGES, 29 CFR Part 1607, provides guidance as to how the Equal Employment Opportunity Commission (EEOC) evaluates selection procedures, formal and informal, in determining whether the procedures violate *Title VII of The Civil Rights act of 1964*, as amended. The UGES specifically provides that selection procedures producing an adverse impact (". . . a selection rate for any racial, ethnic or sex group which is less than four-fifths 4/5 (80%) of the rate for the group with the highest rate") constitute a violation of Title VII unless that procedure is validated as job-related and consistent with the business necessity. The UGES also provides that, generally, individual components of a selection procedure need not be validated nor will they be challenged if there is no adverse impact for the overall selection process, even if it can be shown that an individual component may, in and of itself, produce an adverse impact.

170

The impact of the ADA on the UGES is relatively straight forward. SECTION 102. DISCRIMINATION provides that:

(b) Construction - as used in subsection (a), the term "discriminate" includes -

(3) utilizing standards, criteria, or methods of administration

(A) that have the effect of discrimination on the basis of disability; or

(B) that perpetuate the discrimination of others who are subject to common administrative control;

(6) using qualification standards, employment tests or other selection criteria that screen out or tend to screen out an individual with a disability or a class of individuals with disabilities unless the standard, test or other selection criteria, as used by the coveted entity, is shown to be job related for the position in question and is consistent with business necessity;

Section 1630.10. Qualification Standards, Tests, and Other Selection Criteria of EEOC's guidelines implementing the ADA specifically states that:

"The *Uniform Guidelines on Employee Selection Procedures* (UGESP) 29 CFR Part 1607 do not apply to *The Rehabilitation Act* and are similarly inapplicable to this part."

Section 504 of *The Rehabilitation Act of 1973*, and the ADA provide that employment practices producing an adverse impact, "may not be used unless the employer demonstrates that the criteria, as used by the employer, are job related to the position to which they are being applied and are consistent with business necessity."

Unlike the ADA and its substantive regulations, CRA '91 contains no reference to the UGES. A draft of a statement from the White House designed to coincide with President Bush's signing of the new law called for complete elimination of the UGES. After circulating the draft statement and obtaining adverse reaction from civil rights leaders and proponents of the new law, the President substantially revised his remarks to eliminate any references to UGES and their continued validity under the CRA '91.

In a follow-up conversation with the Regional Attorney for the

Cleveland district office of the EEOC, the Regional Attorney stated that to his knowledge, EEOC would continue to interpret the UGES in the same manner as before CRA '91. However, he did also state that EEOC was still in the process of writing interpretive guidelines to CRA '91. He believed that, under CRA '91, EEOC would look to the bottom line of the selection procedure first and that absent a showing of adverse impact, they would not challenge individual parts of a selection procedure unless they were on their face, illegal. If there was a showing of adverse impact, however, EEOC would look at individual elements of the selection process to determine where the adverse impact was originating.

This approach appears to be entirely consistent with the language and legislative history of the new law. Simply stated, under the CRA '91, there is no prima facie liability unless a complaining party demonstrates that an employer uses a particular employment practice that in fact causes a disparate impact. While the new law codifies prior law, including that established under the Supreme Court's Wards Cove decision to the effect that the plaintiff must identify the particular employment practice producing disparate impact, two exceptions were codified under §105(a). An attack on an employer's "bottom line numbers" is permitted where a company's decision-making process is not capable of separation for analyses. In describing this exception, Senator Dole explained:

"Where a decision-making process includes particular, functionally integrated elements which are components of the same test, those elements may be analyzed as one employment practice. For instance, a 100 question intelligence test may be challenged and defended as a whole: it is not necessary for the plaintiff to show which particular questions have a disparate impact."

137 Cong. Rec. S15472-15478 (Oct. 30, 1991) (emphasis added). Since Senator Dole's comments reflect a testing process may be "defended" as a whole, individual attacks on certain specific questions should not be entertained by the courts.

The critical question then becomes, how does the above application of the ADA and CRA '91 impact the Greentree™ Computer-Assisted Employment Interview (GCEI). We believe the following to be the most likely application of the regulations to the GCEI. Under

CRA '91, an employer is not required to show business necessity where there is no showing of adverse impact. Looking back at the UGES, if there is no adverse impact for the overall selection procedure (i.e., protected class individuals are selected at a similar rate as non-protected class individuals), then the EEOC would not challenge individual components of the selection process. This presumably would include the GCEI or discrete questions within the GCEI, excluding any questions that may be illegal on their face (e.g., questions relating to whether an applicant had previously received workers' compensation for any job-related injuries or illnesses). This would be true even if it could be shown that individual component of the GCEI could theoretically produce an adverse impact.

Practically, if the GCEI does not produce an adverse impact overall, then even attempting to show that individual questions may do so would be next to impossible. To the contrary, the record keeping component of the GCEI and its constant criterion validation process should help an employer in complying with the provisions of CRA '91 and the UGES, and in defending a complaint originating out of the selection procedure.

Consideration of the GCEI under the ADA would take a similar line of analysis. First, it would have to be determined that the GCEI produced an adverse impact in regard to disabled individuals. Obviously, an employer would have to track not only whether the outcome of the GCEI produces an adverse impact, but also whether the methodology for administering the GCEI also has an adverse impact on disabled individuals. As such, if a disabled individual would have a problem in taking the GCEI due to their disability, the employer would have to determine whether a reasonable accommodation would allow the individual to complete the GCEI. This would be no different than making a reasonable accommodation to allow a disabled individual to fill out an employment application.

Under the ADA, the first level analysis would be to determine whether the GCEI overall produces an adverse impact in regards to disabled individuals. Absent a showing of adverse impact, we believe it highly unlikely that the EEOC would challenge or that the courts would entertain challenges to individual components of the selections procedure, including the GCEI or discrete elements of the GCEI.

This does not mean that state fair employment practices agencies or advocacy groups for the disabled would decide to challenge an individual element of the GCEI. However, practically speaking, we believe the likelihood of that happening and any result and exposure to an employer utilizing the GCEI to be slight.

In summary, we believe the conclusions reached in our letter of November 15, 1991, to still be valid. Employers choosing to utilize unstructured and subjective selection procedures will be at a distinct disadvantage to those employers utilizing a structured format such as the GCEI. A structured format utilizing content and criterion validation which also updates itself as to any resulting adverse impact thereby allowing an employer to respond quickly, will place that employer in a distinct advantage if their selection process and decisions are challenged. In addition to lowering risk, the employer utilizing the structured format should obtain a higher quality candidate for consideration for employment.

Please do not hesitate to call if you have any questions regarding the above. We will assist you or your clients on any particular issues with which either you or they may be concerned.

Very truly yours,
Douglas B. Brown
Keith L. Pryatel

DBB:

9150 SOUTH HILLS BOULEVARD • CLEVELAND, OHIO 44147-3599
CLEVELAND (216) 838-8800 • AKRON (216) 253-5500
TELEFAX (216) 838-8805

THE COMPUTER-ASSISTED EMPLOYMENT INTERVIEW AFTER FOURTEEN YEARS

AN INTERVIEW WITH DR. BROOKS MITCHELL

NOTE: In March 1978, an applicant for a sewing operator job at Corbin, Ltd., was asked to answer some pre-employment questions by entering information directly into an Apple II computer. The questions were biographical in nature and an addendum to a Weighted Application Blank process designed by Dr. Brooks Mitchell to reduce employee turnover for Corbin, Ltd. This young female job applicant was the first person ever to be interviewed for employment using a computer.

Q. Dr. Mitchell, how did you get the idea for a computerized employment interview?

A. It took a gradual evolution of thought and experience augmented by education, observation, and common sense. It wasn't a light bulb that flashed in my head one night.

Q. How did it start?

A. Corbin, Ltd. was having employee turnover problems and retained me to conduct a traditional Weighted Application Blank (WAB) study which essentially scored paper-and-pencil job application blanks to predict employee longevity. I was aware of problems with the WAB process that I felt could be solved by use of the microcomputer.

Q. What were some problems with WABs?

A. The biggest problem was that job application blanks contained lim-

175

ited data because they were not designed to collect the depth of information which could be helpful in constructing a statistical profile of the "high turnover" employee. Also, there was the nagging problem of applicant coaching.

Q. Applicant coaching?

A. Applicant coaching is an inadvertent clue dropped by an interviewer which tells a job applicant how to answer a question to score well. This was eliminated by the use of a computer program which required interviewers to enter more information from the application than was necessary. Some of this data was scored by the computer and some was not, allowing the WAB score to remain uncompromised. It would have taken a German cryptographer to decode the real success algorithms.

Q. How did computer use improve the depth of information given by applicants?

A. A computer program was written which asked the applicants to respond directly to a series of multiple choice questions about themselves. My intention was to use this data for subsequent WAB studies, for the data was complete, pertinent, and already in a format ready for processing. I then conducted an analysis to determine the effect the WAB was having on sewing operator tenure at Corbin, Ltd.

Q. What was the result of this analysis?

A. As expected, there was a direct correlation between high WAB scores and low employee turnover. I presented the results to Willeta Damron, the Director of Personnel for Corbin, Ltd. Obviously, she was pleased with the lower turnover, but most of her comments were related to the applicant reactions to the computer questionnaire. I recall Willeta saying, "We are amazed at how much people like this process and how honest they are in their responses."

Q. Did this surprise you?

A. Sure. I was worried that applicants would balk at the process or wouldn't be able to operate the computer. I was wrong, just the opposite occurred.

Q. How did this lead to a computerized employment interview?

A. I kept thinking about the follow-up computer questionnaire and how effective it was. Finally, it sank in. Applicants were actually being interviewed by a computer. So, like a lot of things, the discovery was acci-

dental. I was trying to improve the WAB process and created the computer employment interview as a supplement. I am glad I was alert enough to recognize what was going on.

Q. Were you excited?

A. I was exhilarated because I had always known the immense potential of the structured job interview as an element in the employee selection process. But, like the WAB, there were some inherent problems that limited its effectiveness in most business applications I recognized the capacity of the computer to solve many of these problems and thereby to improve the employee selection process.

Q. For example?

A. A structured interview takes a minimum of one and a half hours to conduct properly. Most organizations won't take that much time. Consequently, they fail to gather a lot of important information. The computer interview allows applicants to complete pre-employment interviews by themselves with minimal supervision, thus freeing company employees. Also, the computer can ask more questions in the same amount of time than a human can, thus developing a greater depth of information. This is particularly helpful to line managers who don't have much experience interviewing people and thus frequently fail to ask the right question the right way.

Q. How else is the computer helpful to line managers?

A. The computer interprets the applicant's responses and selects a series of open-ended probe questions. These probe questions are organized into a structured interview format to be asked by the line manager. So, with minimal training (if the manager can read), he or she can conduct a complete and individualized interview of every applicant. Research has consistently demonstrated that when managers do this, they make better hiring decisions.

Q. Why?

A. When you interpret the results of a structured interview, you are dealing with facts and comparing apples to apples. This eliminates much of the subjective decision-making that results from rambling questions asked during a short interview. The structured interview also minimizes the effect of another problem of subjectivity: an applicant's appearance.

Q. Isn't appearance important?

A. Maybe for some jobs, but in the absence of complete and consistent

177

information from a structured interview, research has shown that appearance frequently becomes the_primary factor in the hiring decision. A computer cannot see an applicant and therefore cannot be influenced by appearance.

Q. What did applicants think about the computer interview?

A. Initially, I am sure they were nervous because most of them had never seen a computer before. Once they started the interview they quickly adapted to the computer, and almost all of the applicants reported that they liked the process. This observation has been confirmed by Dr. John Greist, a psychiatrist at the University of Wisconsin-Madison.

Q. What type of research has Dr. Greist conducted regarding the computer interview?

A. Dr. Greist's work involved the use of a computer to interview heart patients and their families. Although Dr. Greist was not studying the computer for job interviews, our conclusions about the computer interview have been almost identical.

Q. What conclusions were these?

A. That people prefer the computer interview to paper-and-pencil interviews and that they give more honest answers to a computer than they do to a human interviewer.

Q. Why would this be?

A. Dr. Greist's research suggests that people prefer a computer interviewer because they don't fear the negative feedback they might get from a human. A study by another researcher concluded that applicants are more honest to a computer because it reduces the need to give socially desirable responses. A computer is free of bias and prejudice. It has no sex, age, race, or annoying mannerisms. It's easy for applicants to respond honestly to this type of interviewer.

Q. What have you observed in "real" job interview situations?

A. The same as the research findings. Applicants like the computer interview and give honest answers to the questions. Over one million applicants have been interviewed for jobs by computers and I am not aware of a single person who has refused to be interviewed or who has even voiced an objection to the process.

Q. What about the issue of applicant honesty?

A. I have consistently observed that applicants are surprisingly can-

did in their responses to questions asked by the computer. My perception is that most applicants want to give honest replies in a job interview, yet they don't feel compelled to give answers to questions they are not asked. I have found it is more difficult to get interviewers to ask a hard question than it is to get interviewees to give honest answers once the question is asked.

Q. Can you give me an example?

A. Sure. In many computer interviews we ask applicants to tell us how long they plan to stay on the job. Some applicants respond, "Less than six months."

Q. Why would an applicant admit they only plan to stay on the job for six months or less?

A. Because the computer asked the question.

Q. After you realized that you had the core of a computer interview program, what did you do next?

A. I began to expand the capabilities of the computer software so that it corresponded more closely to what a structured job interview should be. For example, question branching was added which allowed the computer to completely explore a subject area. Also, the computer was programmed to select and organize individual open-ended probe questions to be asked by the human interviewer. The software has now developed into what is called an expert system.

Q. What is an expert system?

A. An expert computer software system allows experts to enter their unique knowledge about a situation into a program which then will help less knowledgeable people make more accurate decisions. If properly constructed, an expert computer interview program can be developed that will allow the best or most expert company interviewer to interview every job applicant. This is particularly beneficial to companies with multiple field offices that do not have the benefit of professional human resource support.

Q. Does this mean that each company needs to develop their own specific interviews?

A. Yes, of course. All companies have a unique culture which should be reflected by a unique job interview. There is no canned, off-the-shelf solution to effective employee selection.

Q. Is the computer interview used primarily for jobs at the bottom of the organization?

A. That was the initial focus of the process because that is where the most jobs were. Now it has expanded into first level professional sales and management jobs. In one respect, I think the biggest value of the computer interview will be realized at higher levels in the organization.

Q. Why?

A. Although there are fewer jobs at higher levels in the organization, their impact is exponentially increased. It is far more painful to make a mistake in the employment of a department manager than a sales clerk.

Q. Can a computer interview be scored like a test?

A. Yes, but only if a criterion validity study is conducted after the interview has been used for a few months. In fact, the computer creates an ideal mechanism for a criterion validity analysis because the data is complete, pertinent, and stored in a format ready for analysis. Furthermore, the data can be continually monitored and revalidated to reflect changes in hiring criteria.

Q. What is the value of a criterion validity analysis?

A. Companies, especially in volume-hiring situations, can use a valid pre-screening tool which allows them to focus on applicants with the highest probability of success.

Q. What is the future of computer employment interviewing?

A. It will continue to expand rapidly in American organizations. Also, smaller and more powerful computers have opened new possibilities.

Q. What new possibilities?

A. I am intrigued by the possibility of interactive voice and video capabilities. A computer could be programmed to display and describe realistic job situations and ask an applicant to respond. For example, a video could be produced which realistically portrays a sensitive customer service situation and subsequent employee reaction. Job applicants would be asked to respond as to how they would have handled the situation. A follow-up criterion validity analysis would reveal whether or not the response was related to success at the organization. Exciting, isn't it?

Q. Do you think a computer will ever be able to completely replace a human interviewer?

A. No, not in my lifetime, because so much of a successful hiring depends on a human interviewers being able to bring his or her specific knowledge, skills, and judgments to an interview. The computer can screen applicants and suggest areas that the human interviewer may want to explore further, but it is not yet able to apply the more intuitive human element that necessarily exists in interview situations.